Hardening Your Heart Toward God

Pharaoh's Journey to Destruction

All Bible references used are from the King James Bible
unless otherwise noted.

Written in October, 2017.

Acknowledgments

I have wanted to write this book for a long time. It was always on the top of the list of books I wanted to put into print at some point in my life. That time has finally arrived and I grateful to the Lord that He has given me the opportunity to make it happen. He taught me these truths many years ago; but the Lord, in the middle of writing this book, showed me a fresh insight that I had never seen before. You will find that in Chapter Six.

I want to give my Lord and Savior all the glory for any good that comes as a result of this work. He alone is worthy and I praise Him for His grace and mercy that is continually being poured out on me. There is no greater thing than knowing Jesus!

I want to thank my beautiful wife, Kim, for her faithful love and support of my ministry through thirty-eight years of marriage. I am so blessed to have her by my side. Our four kids (Amy, Nathan, Stacy, and Julie) have also been a source of great encouragement to me through the almost forty years of being a pastor. They and their families continue to serve the Lord which makes Kim and me extremely grateful.

I have had the privilege of serving an absolutely wonderful congregation of saints for over seventeen years at Calvary Baptist Church in San Angelo, Texas. They have encouraged me through all those years with their prayers, their faithfulness, their desire to reach out beyond the walls of our building with the gospel, and their eagerness to hear the word of God. Being their pastor continues to be one of the best things I have ever been able to do. They have allowed me to stretch my faith and expand my ministry. Thank you, church family, for blessing my life and my family's life in so many ways.

Finally, I want to express my thanks to some people who have read through my manuscript, chapter by chapter, and helped me to correct some mistakes along the way. Spell Check does not catch everything; and so, I am grateful to those that took time to do this. James McElroy, one of my church members, read every word of my book. He found something that needed to be corrected in almost every chapter—or maybe it was every chapter. I was amazed at some of the little things I missed. He also would let me know what a good job I was doing. At least I know that there is one person out there that likes my book!

A pastor friend, Mike Dixon, also read through my manuscript and made some pertinent suggestions that would hopefully improve this book. I appreciate his encouragement and support.

My wife, Kim, helped me to get the grammar and words right. Another one of my church members, Mary Nell Lane, read through my manuscript and offered her comments. I appreciate those that came alongside to make this book read a little more smoothly. It really is a great help to writers like me.

To God be the glory!

Preface

*For they considered not the miracle of the loaves:
for their heart was hardened.*   Mark 6:52

You know the story well. It's the feeding of the 5,000. It's the only miracle (other than the resurrection of Jesus) that is recorded in all four gospels. I learned this story as a young boy growing up in Sunday School and a Royal Ambassador at a country church in my home town; but it wasn't until recently that I learned about a certain group of people who got to eat the bread and fish at that miraculous, unscripted and unplanned dinner-on-the-grounds and developed a hard heart (not heart burn). How could that be possible?

When you consider the scope and magnificence of this event, how could it not lead to anything except a strong faith in Jesus Christ? Who else could have taken five loaves and two fish and feed such a multitude? Who else but one from God could perform such a feat?[1] What other conclusion could one draw; but somehow, through this incredible feast provided by Jesus, hard hearts were formed. If you did not know already you need to know now. Having a hard heart is a dangerous thing!

The writer of Proverbs put it like this: "He, that being often reproved hardeneth his neck, shall suddenly be destroyed, and that without remedy" (29:1). This is serious stuff! I do not know about you; but as for me, I do not ever want to have a hard heart toward the Lord Jesus Christ and/or His word. The consequences are way too great—the price is too high to pay for having my heart hardened to the Spirit of God.

---

[1] Nicodemus recognized that Jesus had to be from God based on His miracles. "…no man can do these miracles that thou doest, except God be with him." John 3:2.

That is one reason I have written this book. Many years ago, the Lord showed me some principles in the Exodus story about the process of hardening a heart. These principles come more specifically from the battle between the servant of God, Moses, and his foe, Pharaoh. I discovered that this Egyptian leader went through several stages—stages that are clearly defined in the Bible that tell us just exactly how his heart became so hardened toward God. We all know what it cost Pharaoh in the end. He paid a terrible price for his resistance to a holy God—a price he never thought he would have to pay; but he had no choice. His heart was hardened to the fullest extent. God had already decreed what would take place and His word could not be changed.

In the pages that unfold before us, I want to take you through the process of hardening a heart. While some of these steps may occur in various order in an individual's life, they will all be present at some point in the process unless repentance takes place. That being said, there seems to always be the same starting point that leads, if not corrected, to an end that is costlier than that individual would want to pay.

May the Lord help each of us to search our own hearts and stop the gears of hardening the heart from turning before it is too late!

Table of Contents

Chapter One: The Foundation

The heart is deceitful above all things, and desperately wicked: who can know it? Jeremiah 17:9

I read the story of our Lord sitting around the table with His disciples at the Last Supper and see a living illustration of the verse above. Do you recall what Jesus said? "Verily I say unto you, One of you which eateth with me shall betray me."[2] That statement no doubt came as a great surprise to those gathered around for the pre-crucifixion, Passover Celebration; but it is what they asked that shows us the uncertainty of their heart.

Remember that at this point, they had been following Jesus day after day for over three years. They had eaten hundreds of meals with Him, walked down miles and miles of dusty roads with Him leading the way, heard scores of sermons from his mouth, and had ministered side by side with Him during those years of discipleship training. They had watched Him feed the hungry, heal the sick, raise the dead, and shower countless numbers with the love of God. Their devotion and commitment to Him should have been unshakeable by now but the Scriptures record an amazing response to Jesus' statement. "And they began to be sorrowful, and to say unto him one by one, Is it I? and another said, Is it I?"[3]

Did you catch that? "One by one" they asked the same question. We are talking about the apostle John, the disciple that Jesus loved,[4] wondering if he would be the one to betray his Master. There is

---

[2] Mark 14:18.

[3] Mark 14:19.

[4] We find all of the references to "the disciple whom Jesus loved" in the book of John (John 13:23, John 19:26, John 20:2 and John 21:7, John 21:20).

impetuous Peter who in just a few verses later in Mark's account will tell Jesus that even if everyone else ran away and left Jesus, there would be no way he would ever do that.[5] Then there is James, the third disciple in that inner circle of the closest companions of Christ. He, too, ponders Jesus' words, not knowing if he would be the one to do the unthinkable: betray his Lord.

I find it interesting to talk about what they did not say as well. No disciple—not one single man in that band of Christ-followers—said, "I bet it is Judas!"[6] Had Judas hidden his secret agenda from them that well? Was he able to put on such a "Christian face" that they never suspected he was capable of what he was about to do? Apparently so, but that is not the real issue here.

All twelve disciples show us the heart that indeed is, as Jeremiah puts it, "desperately wicked." The hearts of these men were so untrustworthy and wicked that they were completely unsure of their ability to stay true to their Master. These doubting hearts testify to the acute need for us to heed the command given in Proverbs 4:23: "Keep thy heart with all diligence; for out of it are the issues of life."

According to *Strong's Concordance*, the Hebrew word "keep" means to guard or watch over something. Since the verb "keep" is a command, this is something we must do; but the difficulty comes when we understand that we must guard something that is, as Jeremiah writes, "deceitful above all things, and desperately wicked." We have our work

---

[5] Mark 14:27-29.

[6] It is to be noted that Judas did not say, "It is I. I am the one." The guilty one seldom wants to confess his guilt. Adam did not want to admit his sin in the Garden of Eden. Man is the same way today.

cut out for us; and in the context of this book, we have to guard our heart against it becoming hard to the things of God. (It is at this point I cry out, "Help, Lord!)

What Is A Hard Heart?

Before we get to the actual process of hardening the heart, we need to know what a hard heart is. Of course, the secular sources define it in a way that may or may not relate to the Biblical principle we need to grasp; but I find it good to see what others say.

Mirriam Webster explains hard-hearted as "lacking in sympathetic understanding."[7] Dictionary.com defines it as "unfeeling; unmerciful; pitiless."[8] As you can see, these really do not describe the hard heart we find revealed in the Scriptures. However, *Baker's Evangelical Dictionary of Biblical Theology* gives a solid description of one. "Hardness of heart...describes a negative condition in which the person ignores, spurns, or rejects the gracious offer of God to be a part of his or her life."[9] That brings us closer to where we want to be; but to get us to a more succinct picture of this kind of heart, I want to look at some Biblical words that will help us gain this understanding.

---

[7] "Hard–hearted." Merriam-Webster.com. Merriam-Webster, n.d. Web. 15 June 2017.

[8] Hardhearted. (n.d.). Dictionary.com Unabridged. Retrieved June 15, 2017 from Dictionary.com website http://www.dictionary.com/browse/hardhearted.

[9] Walter A. Elwell. "Entry for 'Hardening, Hardness of Heart'". "Evangelical Dictionary of Theology". 1997. June 15, 2017.j

There are three Hebrew words in the Old Testament, found in eighteen verses in the Exodus account, that are translated in one form or another as the word "harden."[10] There are only slight variations in their meanings; and therefore, they are synonymous. The first word is *chazaq*,[11] which means to make rigid, make hard, or grow rigid. The second word is *kabad*.[12] It means to make heavy, make dull, make unresponsive, and to be heavy, insensible, or dull. The third word, used only once in the Exodus account (Exodus 7:3), is *qashah*;[13] and it means to make hard, to make stiff, or to make stubborn.

This is the Hebrew word used in the Proverbs 29:1 text: "He, that being often reproved hardeneth *(qashah)* his neck, shall suddenly be destroyed, and that without remedy." It is interesting to note that a form of this third Hebrew word *(qasheh)* is translated as "hardhearted" in Ezekiel 3:7; and when combined with the Hebrew word for "neck," we find this two-word combination translated as "stiff-necked." In all six places this translation appears, this descriptive phrase is directed to the Hebrew children (Exodus 32:9; 33:3, 5; 34:9; Deuteronomy 9:6; 9:13). What happened to Pharaoh's heart (as we will see in this book) is exactly what happened to the hearts of the people Moses was attempting to lead

---

[10] The source of my information comes from www.blueletterbible.org and its use of *Strong's Exhaustive Concordance.*

[11] *Chazaq* (H2388) is used in Exodus 4:21; 7:13, 22; 8:19; 9:12, 35; 10:20, 27; 11:10; 14:4, 8, 17.

[12] *Kabad* (H3513) is used in Exodus 8:15, 32; 9:7, 34; 10:1.

[13] *Qashah* is translated as "harden" or "hardened" eleven other times in the rest of the Old Testament.

4

into the Promised Land. They did not get there overnight. They went through a process. It is that process we will begin looking at in the next chapter.

Chapter Two: The Process Begins

*And Pharaoh said, Who is the LORD, that I should obey
his voice to let Israel go? I know not the LORD,
neither will I let Israel go.* Exodus 5:2

With this verse, the process of hardening the heart begins; but
before I expound on this, let us go back to the beginning of this story—
one I am sure you know quite well.[14] Our narrative commences with the
birth of Moses, the man who would one day be the great leader of the
Hebrew people. He had an unusual start—had to be hidden after being
born. It was not that Moses was an unwanted baby. Pharaoh had decreed
that every Hebrew male child be cast into the river and drown (something
about a population explosion among the Hebrews seem to bother
Pharaoh).

God then interjected one of His miraculous and sovereign plans
into the situation. Moses is found floating in a small basket in the river by
Pharaoh's daughter; and before you can turn the page in your Bible, he is
being raised by his own mother in the court of Pharaoh! One day, when
Moses was forty years of age, he got a little anxious about fulfilling God's
plan for his life. He killed an Egyptian and ended up fleeing for his life to
a desert place in Midian. It is there, some forty years later, that Moses is
going to receive a divine call that will literally change the future of the
Hebrew people forever.

What was it God said? "I have surely seen the affliction of my
people which are in Egypt, and have heard their cry" (Exodus 3:7). Praise
God that He cares for His people! The Lord spoke again out of that

---

[14] The story of Moses' life begins in Exodus 2 and continues throughout the rest
of the Pentateuch.

burning but not consumed bush and told Moses, "Come now therefore, and I will send thee unto Pharaoh, that thou mayest bring forth my people the children of Israel out of Egypt" (v. 10).

After working through a few objections, being armed with the name of God and His power, and packing his bags, Moses set out to confront the leader of Egypt about letting God's people go. Before he left, however, the Lord had one more thing to say to him. "And the Lord said unto Moses, When thou goest to return into Egypt, see that thou do all those wonders before Pharaoh, which I have put in thine hand." That was the good news; but the bad news was to follow: "but I will harden *(chazaq)* his heart, that he shall not let the people go" (Exodus 4:21). The Word of the Lord continues:

"And thou shalt say unto Pharaoh, Thus saith the LORD, Israel is my son, even my firstborn: And I say unto thee, Let my son go, that he may serve me: and if thou refuse to let him go, behold, I will slay thy son, even thy firstborn."[15]

It is in these three verses that we are given a foreshadowing of what is going to transpire in the chapters ahead.

1. Moses is going to go before Pharaoh and tell him what God has said.
2. Pharaoh is going to reject Moses and the word of God.
3. By doing so, God is going to make Pharaoh's heart hard.
4. Pharaoh's first-born son will be killed by God.

Of course, we know that there are going to be many one-on one, head-to-head clashes between Moses (and Aaron) and Pharaoh; and it is in

---

[15] Exodus 4:22-23.

those moments that we are going to see the progression from step one to the next step and to the next: the process of hardening the heart.

There is one thing about the word "harden" in Exodus 4:21 that needs to be noted. It is in, what is called in the Hebrew grammar, a PIEL stem. We do not have that form in our English grammar. The best we can do is to put an exclamation mark at the end of a sentence, write a word in large and/or bold print, underline it, and/or write it in *italics*. (We would probably need to do all of these to get the sense of the Hebrew stem.)

When a Hebrew word is in this form, it intensifies the meaning. For example, it would be the difference between a gentle tap on the shoulder and a vicious slap on the back. What God is letting Moses (and us) know is that in hardening Pharaoh's heart, it is not going to be a light thing. He is going to intensify this process; and as the hardening continues, the heart is going to be turned to, in a sense, stone. The unfolding of this will not be a pleasant experience when it is all said and done. This should be cause for alarm. The hardening of the heart is serious business with the Lord.

Now the day came in which Moses, for the first time, went before Pharaoh, no doubt full of bravery and boldness because of his confidence in the Lord. (I often wonder if he actually listened to all that God said.)[16] We read in Exodus 5:1, "And afterward Moses and Aaron went in, and told Pharaoh, Thus saith the LORD God of Israel, Let my people go, that they may hold a feast unto me in the wilderness." Can you picture his

---

[16] Check out Moses' reaction to Pharaoh's response in Exodus 5:22-23. He questions why God even sent him on this mission. He accuses God of treating them in an evil manner.

great courage? "Pharaoh, I am telling you what the LORD God said and you better listen up!"

Did the king listen? Absolutely not! "Who is the LORD, that I should obey his voice to let Israel go? I know not the LORD, neither will I let Israel go."[17] Little did Pharaoh know that by making that statement and saying no to God that he set in motion some gears that would keep turning in his heart and one day result in the death of his first-born son.

What is that first step in the process of doing this? (I'm glad you asked!) DISOBEYING THE WORD OF GOD. The very first time we disobey God and His word, we start the process of hardening our heart toward Him. We begin a journey that, if we reach its final destination, we will discover that we will regret having boarded that train. Saying "no" to God of the universe may seem like a small thing—a baby step; but once we disobey Him, make no mistake about it, that step has been taken. Only a repentant heart can stop the heart-hardening gears from turning.

We have all been here. We heard a sermon and knew God was speaking to our hearts but when the invitation was given, we were able to stand strong and not give in to the conviction of the Holy Spirit. We have sensed in our heart that the Lord was nudging us to do something for someone and we either ignored the prompting of the Lord or simply told him, "No." We went to a camp, a retreat, a seminar, a conference, or any other number of spiritual events and left with a commitment to "attack hell with a water pistol;" and by the time we arrived back home, we failed to take the gun out of the holster.

---

[17] Exodus 5:2.

9

The illustrations could go on and on but the end result is the same. We disobeyed the word of God; and that, my friends, is where the process of hardening the heart begins—every single time. We all start this progression at the same place: disobedience. We may not feel like our hearts are starting to turn to stone but they are. Hardening the heart may be a slow process; but as we disobey God, we allow that process to begin its dangerous work.

Is there an area of your life in which you know you are being disobedient to God? If so, you are already in the process of having your heart hardened. You need to stop the wheels now while you realize what is happening. Repent of your disobedience to God and His word and return to Him. I plead with you in the words of Isaiah, the prophet: "Seek ye the LORD while he may be found, call ye upon him while he is near" (Isaiah 55:6).

Chapter Three: The Finger of God

Then the magicians said unto Pharaoh,
This is the finger of God:
and Pharaoh's heart was hardened,
and he hearkened not unto them; as the LORD had said.
Exodus 8:19

By the time we get to this part of the Exodus story, some interesting and miraculous things have been occurring. Moses has offered his complaint to God about Pharaoh not listening and making life much more difficult for his people.[18] Maybe Moses thought God was caught off guard by the king's[19] response or that God would now see things his way and act immediately to force Pharaoh to change his mind. God, Who was not bothered at all by the disobedient king's response, did let Moses know that He had this all under control. Here is His answer to His grumbling servant: "Then the LORD said unto Moses, Now shalt thou see what I will do to Pharaoh: for with a strong hand shall he let them go, and with a strong hand shall he drive them out of his land" (Exodus 6:1).

Much could be said here but suffice it to mention that God lets Moses know that He had cut a covenant[20] with Abraham's seed and He would make sure He kept His word to them. God says, "And I will bring you in unto the land, concerning the which I did swear to give it to Abraham, to Isaac, and to Jacob; and I will give it you for an heritage: I

---

[18] Exodus 5:22-23.

[19] The Lord calls Pharaoh the "king of Egypt" in Exodus 6:11.

[20] Exodus 6:5. God "remembered" His covenant. This is the Abrahamic Covenant that is found in Genesis 15.

11

am the LORD."[21] It's like God saying to Moses, "Moses, I got this—just hang in there."

The great battle of God and Moses versus Pharaoh begins in chapter seven of Exodus and will consist of a series of ten plagues or miracles that take place and eventually lead to the Hebrew children being released from their four-hundred-plus-years of bondage in Egypt. There is a pre-battle confrontation when Moses and Aaron approach the king and throw down the rod of Aaron.[22] It is miraculously transformed into a snake before their eyes. However, the magicians of Pharaoh's court throw down their sticks and they somehow turn into serpents which results in whole lot of snakes slithering on the ground (This is where I run!).

Of course, Aaron's rod swallows up the magicians' rods (or Aaron's snake eats the magicians' snakes) and then the Bible tells us this: "And he [has to be God doing this] hardened Pharaoh's heart, that he hearkened not unto them; as the LORD had said" (Exodus 7:13). This verse gives us insight to something that is going on behind the scenes. The Lord "hardened Pharaoh's heart"—just like He said He would! I know that there are some who find that hard to believe. Their "God" would not do something like that. All I can say is read the text—search out the references that were given earlier. You will discover that the Scriptures declare ten times that the Lord was directly and actively involved in the hardening of Pharaoh's heart.

---

[21] Exodus 6:8.

[22] Exodus 7:10 clearly states that it is Aaron's rod that gets cast down to the ground. Many mistakenly say that it is Moses' stick. See 7:12 as well. It does appear, however, that this will be same rod Moses will use later on in the Exodus account.

We will see that there are three times we learn that Pharaoh hardened his own heart;[23] but we can rest assured, God was personally involved in what was going on here. There is an old saying that goes like this: "The same sun that melts the ice also hardens the clay."[24] I usually say, "The same sun that melts the butter, hardens the clay." I remember running across another way of saying this a while back but do not recall the source. It goes like this: "The same boiling water that softens the potato hardens the egg." You get the picture. God is doing what He does, based on the responsiveness of Pharaoh's heart. If he obeys, his heart will be softened by God; but if he disobeys, the same God will harden his heart. So, we see, it is really a matter of the heart! God does not change in this at all. He is acting within His sovereign and holy nature at all times.

I must get back to the battle before us. God lets Moses know that "Pharaoh's heart is hardened, he refuseth to let the people go" (Exodus 7:14). God then starts the ten-plague battle with turning the waters that are in the river to blood (7:17). We read, "And the fish that was in the river died; and the river stank, and the Egyptians could not drink of the water of the river; and there was blood throughout all the land of Egypt" (7:21). I am quite sure Moses is thinking this is going to get the king's attention—he will change his mind now; but it did not work.

In fact, we are told that "the magicians of Egypt did so with their enchantments: and Pharaoh's heart was hardened, neither did he hearken

---

[23] Exodus 8:15, 32; 9:34.

[24] I have heard and read this statement many times but do not know who gets credit for saying it first.

13

unto them; as the LORD had said" (7:22). This miracle was duplicated by these enchanters in the court of the king and Pharaoh continued his rebellious journey against God.

We come to the second plague: the plague of frogs. "And Aaron stretched out his hand over the waters of Egypt; and the frogs came up, and covered the land of Egypt" (Exodus 8:6). Maybe, just maybe, this would bring Pharaoh to his knees. We know that it did not for we read in the next verse in this passage, verse 7, "And the magicians did so with their enchantments, and brought up frogs upon the land of Egypt." Once again, Pharaoh's men are able to produce the same miracle with their own enchantments. The frogs die out and we read these words: "But when Pharaoh saw that there was respite, he hardened his heart, and hearkened not unto them; as the LORD had said" (8:15). This is the first time we are told that Pharaoh hardens his own heart. We see there are two forces at work turning the gears now: God and Pharaoh. This is not good.

We learned in the last chapter that the first step in the process of hardening your heart is DISOBEYING THE WORD OF GOD. We now arrive at the next step in this process. It is DENYING THE WORK OF GOD. We come to the third plague: lice. "And the LORD said unto Moses, Say unto Aaron, Stretch out thy rod, and smite the dust of the land, that it may become lice throughout all the land of Egypt" (8:16). Aaron obeys God and there is lice everywhere in Egypt! However, now we see a new element in the Exodus story.

Exodus 8:18 tells us, "And the magicians did so with their enchantments to bring forth lice, but they could not: so there were lice upon man, and upon beast." At this point, the magicians can no longer

14

mimic the miracles of God. I am sure they tried every spell in their book of divinations but it was to no avail. They simply could not produce lice in any form or fashion. Listen to what they understood about this situation. "Then the magicians said unto Pharaoh, This is the finger of God" (8:19). Did you catch that? These heathen men recognized that there was a God that was bigger and greater than them and that what had just happened had to be the finger of God.

Jim Crooks writes these words. "You would think some of this would have softened the old Pharaoh's heart. You would think! You would think that after watching the kind of things he was fixin' to see that he would "reconsider his ways and repent" toward God. I mean God declares war on his religious system and beats the slop out of it. I can't imagine a man that has been given more warnings and insights into the power of God than this old fool."[25]

Indeed, one would think Pharaoh should have relented and released the people of God; but he did not. Instead, the Scriptures record, "and Pharaoh's heart was hardened, and he hearkened not unto them; as the LORD had said" (8:19). Pharaoh had disobeyed the word of God and now he denies the work of God. He has now put himself in a situation where the gears of the hardening process are turning a little faster. God has worked faithfully to get his attention. Others around him can see the hand of God but he refuses to give the Lord any credit for what has taken place. His heart is now a little harder—not nearly as soft and pliable as it once might have been.

---

[25] https://jcrooks.wordpress.com/2010/01/24/the-same-sun-that-melts-the-ice-also-hardens-the-clay/.

As time goes on in this Exodus account, there is another instance when Pharaoh ignores the hand of God. We come to the fifth plague, the one in which God puts His hand on the Egyptians' cattle and cause them to die.[26] The livestock disaster begins with an unwritten, but understood, meeting between Moses and the Egyptian leader. These meetings begin with Moses telling him that God has issued the command to let His people go. Of course, Pharaoh's response is one of disobedience. The process of turning his heart to stone continues.

In this particular plague, the Word of the Lord is clear. A refusal to release the people of God will result in a massive disease among your cattle that will bring about their death. However, God points out something about this event. "And the LORD shall sever between the cattle of Israel and the cattle of Egypt: and there shall nothing die of all that is the children's of Israel" (Exodus 9:4).

Thus, the plague begins. Just like God said, the cattle of the Egyptians start dropping like flies to the point that it is recorded that "all the cattle of Egypt died" (Exodus 9:6). This resulted in a large number of dead bovines across the land; but then, Pharaoh did something rather interesting. "And Pharaoh sent, and, behold, there was not one of the cattle of the Israelites dead" (9:7).

The New Living Translation puts it like this. "Pharaoh sent his officials to investigate, and they discovered that the Israelites had not lost a single animal!" What did the king discover? He found out that the God of Moses, Aaron, and Israel did exactly what He said He would do. One has to wonder what Pharaoh thought when the news was brought to his

---

[26] This part of the Exodus story takes place in Exodus 9:7.

palace. No one told him that it was the finger of God but there was no mistake about it. Someone greater than any god of Egypt was in charge!

How did Pharaoh respond? As usual, he continued his rebellion, his disobedience, and his denial of the work of God. "And the heart of Pharaoh was hardened, and he did not let the people go" (Exodus 9:7). No matter what God was doing, the king was not going to relent or repent.

How about you? How often has God tried to get your attention? It was obvious to others what He was trying to do but you ignored the work of God—rejected it—and now your heart is becoming progressively indifferent to the things of God. Maybe He spared your life in a car wreck in which you probably should have died. It could be that you had a death threat from cancer or some other disease but you have somehow survived the scare and have moved on with your life. The financial crisis you were experiencing has been resolved. Through all these things (and more), God tried to get your attention but you failed to see His hand working in your life. You did not heed the voice of God telling you to turn from your way of living and turn to Him. You simply failed to see the "finger of God;" or if you did, you disregarded it.

Do not do that! Stop those gears from turning while you have the opportunity! Think about all that the Lord has done for you. Thank Him for His incredible mercy and for giving you another chance. Take advantage of that second (maybe third or fourth) chance and turn to Him. He loves you and wants to bless you more than you can ever know. I close this chapter with the words of the psalmist from the first part of Psalm 46:10: "Be still, and know that I am God." Do not miss the "finger of God!"

17

Chapter Four: Three Compromises

*We will go three days' journey into the wilderness, and sacrifice to the
LORD our God, as he shall command us.*
Exodus 8:27

Moses knew what God wanted him to do. He knew God's will.
God had made it clear before he ever approached Pharaoh. The words of
the Lord at the burning bush had not been forgotten. "Certainly I will be
with thee; and this shall be a token unto thee, that I have sent thee: When
thou hast brought forth the people out of Egypt, ye shall serve God upon
this mountain" (Exodus 3:12). God's will involved getting these Hebrew
slaves back to the same mountain from which He had spoken with Moses.
The Bible verse below this chapter's heading is only a repetition of what
the Lord had told Moses earlier to speak to the Egyptian king.[27]

The plan was easy enough to understand: rescue the people from
bondage, go on a three-day journey into the wilderness, and sacrifice to
the LORD God. However, Pharaoh's heart was slowly, but surely being
hardened; so, he had other ideas. In the midst of the next series of plagues
(flies, death of the Egyptians' cattle, the boils or sores on the Egyptians,
the fire and hail, the locusts, and the three days of darkness), we discover
another step in the process of hardening the heart.

It all began with DISOBEYING THE WORD OF GOD. Then
came DENYING THE WORK OF GOD. Now we see DISTORTING
THE WAY OF GOD. The one-word phrase of describing this is what we
call "compromising." When you read the Exodus text, you will discover
three different deals Pharaoh offers Moses and his people that are not

---

[27] God's plan for His people is first stated in Exodus 3:18.

18

congruent with God's plan. He, like many today, thought that God's will was negotiable—God's commandments were only suggestions but in no way did they demand his compliance. In his encounters with Moses, he offers three distortions of the way of God.

Distortion #1: Stay in Egypt and Sacrifice

When the swarm of flies came over the land, "Pharaoh called for Moses and for Aaron, and said, Go ye, sacrifice to your God in the land" (Exodus 8:25). Somehow in Pharaoh's mind, this would be sufficient enough to get Moses (and God) off his back. "You can sacrifice," he offers, "but you must stay within the boundaries of Egypt." If Moses' commitment to the word of God was weak, this might have some appeal. After all, God did want His people to worship Him.

However, Moses did not waver! Here was his response: "And Moses said, It is not meet so to do; for we shall sacrifice the abomination of the Egyptians to the LORD our God: lo, shall we sacrifice the abomination of the Egyptians before their eyes, and will they not stone us? We will go three days' journey into the wilderness, and sacrifice to the LORD our God, as he shall command us" (Exodus 8:26-27). Moses clearly understood the Lord's instructions and staying in Egypt to offer sacrifices that would not please Him was not one of the options on the table.

What happens next? The plague of flies is removed even to the extent that "there remained not one"[28] Once again, we see the impact on Pharaoh's heart. "And Pharaoh hardened his heart at this time also, neither

---

[28] Exodus 8:31.

would he let the people go" (8:32). The first compromise was not accepted; but Pharaoh was not finished with playing, "Let's Make A Deal"[29] with Moses and God.

Distortion #2: Just Take Men with You

The battle continues for the freedom of the Israelites. A few of Pharaoh's servants were catching on to what was taking place. They appealed to their king, "How long shall this man be a snare unto us? let the men go, that they may serve the LORD their God: knowest thou not yet that Egypt is destroyed" (Exodus 10:7)? They were willing to get rid of Moses and his people—or at least the men; and that is apparently the only part of their words Pharaoh heard.

Moses and Aaron appear before the king and are asked just who were the ones that were to go and serve the Lord.[30] Moses quickly responded to let him know that they would be leaving "with our young and with our old, with our sons and with our daughters, with our flocks and with our herds" (Exodus 10:9). That certainly did not set well with Pharaoh and after mockingly telling them they could take their little ones with them,[31] he replies with these words. "Not so: go now ye that are men, and serve the LORD; for that ye did desire. And they were driven out from Pharaoh's presence" (10:11).

---

[29] This is the title of an old TV game show that has been revived more recently.

[30] Exodus 10:8. Note that Pharaoh told them to "Go, serve the LORD your God" but there are certainly going to be some stipulations—at least on his part.

[31] Exodus 10:10—another example of Pharaoh's total lack of the fear of the LORD.

The plague of locusts followed. Pharaoh complained, feigned repentance,[32] and of course, refused to let God's people go. His compromise was rejected but his heart became more like stone. After the removal of the locusts, we read these words. "But the LORD hardened Pharaoh's heart, so that he would not let the children of Israel go" (Exodus 10:20). While the seeds of a hardened heart were found internally in the king, God has joined in the process and is going to make sure those seeds bear fruit—not the kind Pharaoh wants but the kind a hard heart produces. The second compromise has also been rejected but the king had one more offer to put on the table.

Distortion #3: You Can Go but Leave Your Animals Behind

The ninth plague has now come upon the land of Egypt. Three days of darkness would permeate and saturate the land. It would be a darkness so great that the Scriptures say it could be "felt."[33] Now that is some kind of darkness! You have to love what you read in Exodus 10:23 in speaking of the Egyptians. "They saw not one another, neither rose any from his place for three days: but all the children of Israel had light in their dwellings." What a miracle!

Getting back to Pharaoh's third distortion, he calls for Moses (no mention of Aaron this time) and says, "Go ye, serve the LORD; only let your flocks and your herds be stayed: let your little ones also go with you" (Exodus 10:24). Here is another proposal set forth by Pharaoh. He will let

---

[32] Pharaoh says, "I have sinned against the LORD your God, and against you" (Exodus 10:16).

[33] Exodus 10:21.

21

all the people of Israel go. After all, is that not what they wanted? Had not Moses said earlier, "Let my people go"?[34] As for their animals—they had to stay behind.

Moses is going to reject this third compromise. He says to the king, "Thou must give us also sacrifices and burnt offerings, that we may sacrifice unto the LORD our God. Our cattle also shall go with us; there shall not an hoof be left behind; for thereof must we take to serve the LORD our God; and we know not with what we must serve the LORD, until we come thither" (Exodus 10:25-26). Moses lets Pharaoh know that when they left Egypt, they were all going; and they would be taking everything they have with them.

Once again, after hearing Moses' words, the wheels spin a little more and Pharaoh's heart continues to be hardened. "But the LORD hardened Pharaoh's heart, and he would not let them go" (10:27). What started with disobedience is still being manifested the same way. Pharaoh DISOBEYED THE WORD OF GOD, DENIED THE WORK OF GOD, and has now DISTORTED THE WAY OF GOD.

Have you ever tried to make a deal with God? Have you ever compromised your faith? I see it all the time. A young girl knows that the man she wants to date is not a Christian but she will tell herself and others that he is not "that bad." A man who knows his habits are both displeasing to God and hurting his family agrees to only quit some of them. We argue that something we do is alright because the Bible does not have a command stating "Thou shalt not..." We call these "gray"

_____

[34] Exodus 5:1.

areas but the word of God only sees things as black and white—sin and righteousness.

It is rather amazing how we can reason away our lack of obedience to the commands of God—even when we know for certain what He has said in His word. Every time we disobey, we make another contribution to the process of developing a hard heart. Each compromise we choose is an indicator telling us that the potential heart-hardening-machinery is alive within us. Stop what you are doing now! Turn from your disobedience. Return to God's word and start walking in obedience. I give you this verse to consider in closing this chapter. "Therefore to him that knoweth to do good, and doeth it not, to him it is sin" (James 4:17).

Chapter Five: You Can't Fool God
But as for thee and thy servants,
I know that ye will not yet fear the Lord God
Exodus 9:30

Jesus was speaking to the Jews at Jerusalem one day during a Passover season. He had just driven a certain group of men out of the temple who were making an illegal profit at this Jewish festive celebration. There were a number of people who believed in Him, especially after seeing His miracles. However, the Scriptures record the following words in John 2:24-25. "But Jesus did not commit himself unto them, because he knew all men, and needed not that any should testify of man: for he knew what was in man."

Did you catch that? "He knew what was *in man*" (emphasis mine). I wonder how often we remember that. Kind of scary, isn't it? The Lord knows what is in me (my heart—my mind). King David came to a place in his life where he learned that truth. "O LORD, thou hast searched me, and known me…thou understandest my thought afar off… and art acquainted with all my ways… For there is not a word in my tongue, but, lo, O LORD, thou knowest it altogether" (Psalm 139:1-4).

The prophet Jeremiah penned these words. "I the LORD search the heart, I try the reins, even to give every man according to his ways, and according to the fruit of his doings" (Jeremiah 17:10). That verse comes right after the one on our hearts being "deceitful above all things, and desperately wicked" (17:9). We learn from these words that our wicked hearts are under the scrutiny and evaluation of God Himself. This is why we need a new heart!

So, God knows everything about us—not just what we are outwardly to others, but what we are inwardly—in our hearts. He knows every word we speak even before we speak it. He knows every thought we have. (Kind of scary, isn't it?) Nothing is hidden from Him. He knows every promise we have made and just how many of them we have failed to keep. He knows every time we have said we were going to be more faithful to Him and instead, have strayed further away.

In other words, you cannot fool God. You can "pull the wool" over a lot of people's eyes, but not His. He is acutely aware of the words we say that are used to bail us out of difficult situations. We have all tried this at one time or another. Pharaoh attempted it with Moses as well. How did that work for him? We will take a look and see.

This part of our story takes place in Exodus, chapter nine. The seventh plague has come upon Pharaoh and the Egyptians. A massive hail storm has pelted the countryside. Along with the hail, "fire ran along upon the ground."[35] Anyone caught outside in this miracle of God would die; and only in the land of Goshen, the campsite of the Israelites, would there be no hail. This is another powerful demonstration of God's judgment and mercy.

Apparently, Pharaoh had more than he could take. Could it be that this storm had finally cracked his hard heart and freedom was near for God's people? Listen to what he says to Moses. "I have sinned this time: the LORD is righteous, and I and my people are wicked" (Exodus 9:27). This sounds pretty good so far—revival must be near! He continues. "Intreat the LORD (for it is enough) that there be no more mighty

---

[35] See Exodus 9:17-26.

thunderings and hail; and I will let you go, and ye shall stay no longer" (9:28).

Glory! Pharaoh has cried, "Uncle." He cannot take it anymore. (It is at this point that I can hear William Wallace in the Mel Gibson movie, *Braveheart,* yelling, "FREEDOM!") The King of Egypt is going to let God's people go! He said so himself.

Not so fast. Remember the first part of this chapter? God knows the heart—even Pharaoh's heart. God had given some insight to Moses about Pharaoh's heart as well. Moses begins with some good news. He tells the king that the hail will end soon. "And Moses said unto him, As soon as I am gone out of the city, I will spread abroad my hands unto the LORD; and the thunder shall cease, neither shall there be any more hail; that thou mayest know how that the earth is the LORD'S" (Exodus 9:29).

His words, however, do not stop there. He goes on to say in the next verse, "But as for thee and thy servants, I know that ye will not yet fear the LORD God." Here, we have another step in the progression of hardening the heart.

This process began with DISOBEYING THE WORD OF GOD. It continued with DENYING THE WORK OF GOD and DISTORTING THE WAY OF GOD. The next step is DISCOUNTING THE WISDOM OF GOD. In other words, we say the right words—make the right promises to get out of trouble; but as soon as the trouble is gone, we never deliver on our word and think that God will not notice. Do we think God is only concerned with our words and not our actual commitment to keep them?

26

Was Moses right about the words of the king? We read on in the passage before us. "And Moses went out of the city from Pharaoh, and spread abroad his hands unto the LORD: and the thunders and hail ceased, and the rain was not poured upon the earth. And when Pharaoh saw that the rain and the hail and the thunders were ceased, he sinned yet more, and hardened his heart, he and his servants. And the heart of Pharaoh was hardened, neither would he let the children of Israel go; as the LORD had spoken by Moses" (Exodus 9:33-35).

Notice that Moses kept his word. The hail was stopped but Pharaoh failed to keep his promise. He hardened his own heart with his sinfulness (his lie and continual disobedience); and because of that, we are told that "the heart of Pharaoh was hardened" (35). His words were meaningless and empty. His promise was void and vain. God knew that. Moses knew that. He may have thought he was smarter than God and His servant, but he was wrong; and what happened because of this? His heart continued to grow harder and harder; and perhaps, occurring more rapidly. Soon Pharaoh's heart would be stone cold to God.

Pharaoh's promise to release the Israelites is another in a long line of similar statements that have come to be known as "fox-hole promises." "We've all heard about fox-hole promises—promises that are made to God when we are caught in a difficult situation or when our back is against the wall. And as soon as the problem passes, the promise we made to God in our hour of desperate need is quickly forgotten."[36]

Do we really believe we can fool God? Maybe Pharaoh did, but do we? The Apostle Paul makes a statement in Galatians 6:7 that we all need

---

[36] http://www.actsweb.org/articles/article.php?i=1082&d=2&c=2.

to heed. "Be not deceived; God is not mocked: for whatsoever a man soweth, that shall he also reap." We cannot fool God. He knows our hearts. We can say whatever we want but the Lord still examines our heart. He discerns whether or not we are being honest.

As a pastor, I have seen this countless number of times. People get in a financial jam; and in their desperation, they beg God to help them out as they make promises to walk with Him more faithfully if He will just hear their prayers. God intervenes and their need is met, sometimes in abundance; and then amazingly, these people drop out of church.

I am called to the bedside of someone who is desperately sick; but they have promised to get back in church and serve God, if He will heal them. The healing comes and away they go—away from the Lord and the church, never to honor the promise they made to God.

A family crisis has arisen and the father and/or the mother cries out to God and asks for help. Again, promises are made to turn back to God if He will just bring the prodigal child home or the wayward son back— bring the runaway daughter out of the hands of the devil and return her back to the family. The miracle is done. The family is whole. The promise is forgotten. God is still forsaken.

The scenarios may change but the pattern does not. I am amazed at how many people DISCOUNT THE WISDOM OF GOD; and as that is done, hearts are becoming more like stone. The only hope is true repentance and that is much more than just saying words or making a promise. It is a true commitment to God and His ways. It is a matter of the heart. I close this chapter with these great words of the psalmist: "Search me, O God, and know my heart: try me, and know my thoughts:

28

And see if there be any wicked way in me, and lead me in the way everlasting" (Psalm 139:23-24).

Chapter Six: Before Honor Comes Humility

And Moses and Aaron came in unto Pharaoh, and said unto him,
Thus saith the LORD God of the Hebrews,
How long wilt thou refuse to humble thyself before me?
let my people go, that they may serve me.
Exodus 10:3

The Bible records twice, in the Book of Proverbs, "before honor is humility."[37] It would have been good for Pharaoh had he understood those words and would also be good for us if we would heed them. One of these proverbial principles contains another statement that tells us exactly where our Exodus story is headed—at least for the prideful king of Egypt. "Before destruction the heart of man is haughty."[38]

Haughtiness—the arrogant spirit of a man that exalts himself above God and everyone else. We see this spirit in the very first encounter between Moses and Pharaoh. Remember how the king responded to God's command to let His people go? "Who is the LORD, that I should obey his voice to let Israel go? I know not the LORD, neither will I let Israel go."[39] As the story goes on, Pharaoh's proud and conceited heart continues to turn the gears; and his heart more quickly proceeds on the deadly path of destruction as promised by God.

This is just another step along the way in the process of hardening the heart. In reality, it is a part of all the other steps. Each time God's word is rejected, Pharaoh's pride is one of the root causes for him reacting this way. After all, he is the King of Egypt. Why should he take orders

---

[37] Proverbs 15:33 and Proverbs 18:12.

[38] Proverbs 18:12.

[39] Exodus 5:2.

from anyone else? Everyone must bow to his wishes and his orders. He is the king.

By the way, all of us exhibit that same attitude at times. We do not want anyone, even God, telling us what to do. We want to be our own boss. We want to rule our own lives and sit on our little throne. We all too often enjoy being the king; but if we are going to bask in the glory of God's blessings, we must step down from that throne and let the Lord Jesus Christ take His rightful place there. He is The King!

We pick up the Exodus story with another word from God about what He is doing (and already has done) with Pharaoh. We read, "And the LORD said unto Moses, Go in unto Pharaoh: for I have hardened his heart, and the heart of his servants, that I might shew these my signs before him: and that thou mayest tell in the ears of thy son, and of thy son's son, what things I have wrought in Egypt, and my signs which I have done among them; that ye may know how that I am the LORD" (Exodus 10:1-2). That clay heart of the king is being hardened by the sunlight and heat of God's sovereign will.

I do not want to just run past what God tells Moses here. We often think that the only person having a problem with knowing God is Pharaoh and the citizens of Egypt, but did you catch what the Lord said? God wants the Israelites to be able to pass down the Exodus story from generation to generation for one specific reason: "that ye may know how that I am the LORD" (Exodus 10:2). God wants there to be no doubt in His own people's eyes just who He is. He is the LORD! He knew His people would continue to struggle with that truth with every new generation of the Israelites.

31

When you think about the complete Bible story, from Genesis to Revelation, you discover that this is where the whole thing is going. All history will culminate in one great declaration of who Jesus is! In addressing this issue, Paul writes these powerful prophetic words. "Wherefore God also hath highly exalted him, and given him a name which is above every name: That at the name of Jesus every knee should bow, of things in heaven, and things in earth, and things under the earth; And that every tongue should confess that Jesus Christ is Lord, to the glory of God the Father."[40] (I admit, it chased a rabbit here; but is a glorious one!)

Again, back to our story. After hearing from God in the first two verses of chapter ten of Exodus, Moses and Aaron approach the Egyptian king. This time, he gets down to the real source of Pharaoh's problem. "How long wilt thou refuse to humble thyself before me?" It is clear from Exodus 10:3 that the "me" is not Moses or Aaron. It is God. The truth has been told. Pharaoh is full of pride—empty of humility. He has a haughty, arrogant spirit; and with that understanding, we come to another step in the heart-hardening process.

We have seen Pharaoh DISOBEYING THE WORD OF GOD, DENYING THE WORK OF GOD, DISTORTING THE WAY OF GOD, and DISCOUNTING THE WISDOM OF GOD. Now we see him DEFYING THE WORTH OF GOD. This defying of God's worth is not a single act that occurs at one point of time. It is the general attitude of the heart of someone who has no desire to do the will of God. That describes

---

[40] Philippians 2:9-11.

the king perfectly. He refused to recognize the authority, the power, and even the existence of Jehovah God.

As far as he is concerned, the God of Moses has no worth. He does not value God in any way at all and he certainly never intends to obey this "worthless" God of Israel. (This is Pharaoh's opinion of God— not this author's.) His heart is far from Jehovah. This is displayed in his actions and his responses to Moses. It is evidenced by the words he speaks and it does not matter what goes on around him or what others may think. We see this as chapter ten continues.

Moses and Aaron let the king know that if he persists in his refusal to let God's people go, there would be a great plague of locusts. These locusts would not be just your every-day kind of locusts. Moses and Aaron said, they "shall cover the face of the earth, that one cannot be able to see the earth: and they shall eat the residue of that which is escaped, which remaineth unto you from the hail, and shall eat every tree which groweth for you out of the field: And they shall fill thy houses, and the houses of all thy servants, and the houses of all the Egyptians; which neither thy fathers, nor thy fathers' fathers have seen, since the day that they were upon the earth unto this day" (Exodus 10:5-6). Now that is a plague of locusts!

Logic and reason tells us that with this kind of threat, a change of heart needs to be considered at the least. The seed of the fear of the Lord ought to begin to sprout at this point in Pharaoh's life; but clearly, it does not. However, his pride stands as a brick wall and prevents him from listening to God and even listening to his servants. Listen to what they say. "And Pharaoh's servants said unto him, How long shall this man be a snare unto us? let the men go, that they may serve the LORD their God: knowest thou not yet that Egypt is destroyed?" (Exodus 10:7).

They had come to recognize who God is. These scared servants understood that something was going on that was much bigger than them. Their only hope of survival was to get rid of Moses and the Israelites. They feared the total destruction of Egypt; however, their pleas and words fell on deaf ears. Pharaoh had once again refused to humble himself before God. His heart was growing harder—his pride getting greater—his destruction was drawing nearer.

The locusts came and it was bad—really bad. "And the locusts went up over all the land of Egypt, and rested in all the coasts of Egypt: very grievous were they; before them there were no such locusts as they, neither after them shall be such. For they covered the face of the whole earth, so that the land was darkened; and they did eat every herb of the land, and all the fruit of the trees which the hail had left: and there remained not any green thing in the trees, or in the herbs of the field, through all the land of Egypt" (Exodus 10:14-15). It could not get much worse than this.

How would mighty Pharaoh respond to this plague? Once again, he showed his disdain for God and continued to defy God's worth. He hastily called for Moses and Aaron; and then, he feigned repentance, proving once more his total lack of respect for the God of Israel. "I have sinned against the LORD your God, and against you. Now therefore forgive, I pray thee, my sin only this once, and intreat the LORD your God, that he may take away from me this death only" (Exodus 10:16-17).

Surely no one believes he meant those words. He had already discounted the wisdom of God before and now he is doing it again; and this time, with an in-your-face kind of attitude. The Scriptures point out that "God is not mocked."[41] The NET Bible version of this phrase says it like this: "God will not be made a fool." Certainly, Pharaoh thought his words would do just that—fool God, fool Moses, fool Aaron, and fool anyone else who would hear him speak. He was only deceiving himself.

"And the LORD turned a mighty strong west wind, which took away the locusts, and cast them into the Red sea; there remained not one locust in all the coasts of Egypt" (Exodus 10:19). The locusts came, the damage was great, the locusts were taken away, and Pharaoh continued on his path to destruction. His lack of humility was sealing his own fate. God would make sure of that. "But the LORD hardened Pharaoh's heart, so that he would not let the children of Israel go" (10:20).

Eight plagues had come and eight plagues had gone. God's people were still in bondage and Pharaoh was still disobeying God while his heart continually and most assuredly was turning to stone. God would certainly not be mocked. His word would be proven to be right. Pride does indeed come before destruction and a "haughty spirit before a fall."[42] That is what the word of God tells us and His word is always the truth.[43]

How about you, my reader friend? Is there an area of your life in which you are full of pride and you refuse to humble yourself before God?

---

[41] See Galatians 6:7.

[42] Proverbs 16:18.

[43] Jesus declares in John 17:17, "Sanctify them through thy truth: thy word is truth."

Pride is a killer! You have probably heard it said before that the middle letter of "pride" and the middle letter of "sin" is the letter "I." That sums up the foundation of both words. They both occur because of an "I" problem. I want to be in charge. I want to call the shots. I want to be the boss. I do not want anyone else telling me what to do—no, not even God. That reminds me of the "I" problem Satan displayed in Isaiah 14.[44]

That's never the right attitude. If left unchecked, it will always get us in trouble. The Scriptures guarantee it. I mentioned this verse earlier but I want to repeat it here. "Before destruction the heart of man is haughty, and before honor is humility."[45] Pharaoh's life proves this. You certainly do not want your life to duplicate this process. Repentance is definitely in order.

The prophet Obadiah wrote some powerful words about the sin of pride. "The pride of thine heart hath deceived thee, thou that dwellest in the clefts of the rock, whose habitation is high; that saith in his heart, Who shall bring me down to the ground? Though thou exalt thyself as the eagle, and though thou set thy nest among the stars, thence will I bring thee down, saith the LORD."[46] Man's pride certainly does not go unnoticed by the Lord.

Even the New Testament addressed this issue. Two times, we read these words. "God resisteth the proud, but giveth grace unto the

---

[44] Satan's five "I will" statements are found in Isaiah 14:13-14.

[45] Proverbs 18:12.

[46] Obadiah 1:3-4.

humble."[47] I do not know about you but one of the last things I want to happen in my life is for God to resist me. We have seen through the pages of this book that God resisted Pharaoh. He stood adamantly against this prideful king. I do not want that to be my story. Rather, I want to do all I can to make this closing verse an ongoing and operational attitude of my heart: "Humble yourselves in the sight of the Lord, and he shall lift you up."[48] I pray that this is your desire as well.

May the Lord give us all the grace we need to stay humble before Him that we may be lifted up and that our heart will stay soft and pliable before our Almighty God!

---

[47] James 4:6 and I Peter 5:5.

[48] James 4:10.

Chapter Seven: Get Out of Here!
And Moses said, Thou hast spoken well,
I will see thy face again no more.
Exodus 10:29

Darkness—it can be frightening. It can be very dark as well. In 2006, my church built a Fellowship Center. The bathrooms are down a hallway; and to get to either one of them, you have to go through two doors. The first door puts you into a mini-foyer. The second one puts you in the actual room.

There are no windows in the bathrooms or the small foyers. Now if you happen to go through those two doors at night and no lights have been turned on, you are in the dark—pitch dark. There is not even a hint of outside light coming in from underneath the bottom of the doors. Total darkness fills the air and fully blinds anyone there! You cannot see the back of your hand (or even the front).

This kind of darkness is not something many, if any, would want to experience; but Egypt did during plague number nine. The darkness was so deep that, as was mentioned in a previous chapter, it could be felt![49] The Hebrew word for "felt" here has the idea of groping or reaching out and feeling something. Darkness that can be felt—that is a deep darkness; and in itself, would be quite scary.

To make matters worse, the Scriptures record this fact. "And Moses stretched forth his hand toward heaven; and there was a thick darkness in all the land of Egypt three days" (Exodus 10:22). Can you imagine being in darkness like this for three days? Notice that this verse

---

[49] See Exodus 10:21.

calls it "thick darkness." The Hebrew word for "thick" here is used in Amos 5:20 to describe the Day of the Lord. "Shall not the day of the LORD be darkness, and not light? even very dark [thick], and no brightness in it?"

There is one more thing about this darkness we need to note. During that three-day period of extreme darkness, the Bible records that the Egyptians "saw not one another, neither rose any from his place for three days" (Exodus 10:23). Since we read that they went three days without seeing one another, the implication seems to be that they did not even have light from their lanterns, torches, candles, or any other source by which they would be able to receive light. This is much worse than living in constant darkness at the North Pole during the dead of Winter!

Even when there was a sunrise, they had no light. At high noon, there was still no light. If a full moon would have been in the sky, the Egyptians still would not have had even a single glimmer of light. There must have been a horrific feeling of fear and panic throughout all of Egypt; but listen to these words. "But all the children of Israel had light in their dwellings" (Exodus 10:23). Praise God for another miracle as He continues to watch over His people even though they were yet in bondage to Pharaoh! However, things would be changing soon. The king's heart is not completely hardened but it is well on its way to that final mark.

I have spent quite a bit of time on this plague of darkness because I want you to understand the setting of the final encounter between Pharaoh and Moses, and the last step in the process of hardening the heart. As I mentioned in Chapter Two, the first step in this process is always the same: DISOBEYING THE WORD OF GOD. The other four steps

(DENYING THE WORK OF GOD, DISTORTING THE WAY OF GOD, DISCOUNTING THE WISDEOM OF GOD, and DEFYING THE WORTH OF GOD) along the way can be in any order and can mix and mingle among themselves. This final step could occur at any time; but as the gears of the heart are slowing turning and producing a heart of stone, it is most likely to appear toward the end of the whole process. What is this step? We will see it as we continue the story.

The three days of intense darkness apparently did something to Pharaoh. I am thinking he could stand it no longer. He called for Moses once again and offered him the compromise of leaving Egypt but not taking the animals.[50] Of course, Moses rejected this offer; and the Scriptures record that "the LORD hardened Pharaoh's heart, and he would not let them go" (Exodus 10:27).

This was the proverbial final straw. Pharaoh's anger was kindled (not mentioned in the text but you can certainly hear it); and he said to Moses, "Get thee from me, take heed to thyself, see my face no more; for in that day thou seest my face thou shalt die" (Exodus 10:28). In this statement, we see the last and final step in the process of hardening the heart: DISAVOWING[51] THE WORKER OF GOD. In other words, the king says rather vehemently, "Get out of here now; because if I ever see your face again, I am going to kill you!"

This is where we discover a man can come to a place in his life that he does not want anyone or anything around him that would even

---

[50] See page 21 and the section on Distortion #3.

[51] To disavow someone is to refuse to acknowledge or accept them; to repudiate them. Certainly, this is Pharaoh's attitude toward Moses at this point.

40

remotely remind him of the word of God or God Himself. That is a hard heart! I have seen this myself in four decades of being a pastor. Some people simply do not want the preacher around them. It is not that I am not a likeable guy (I know I am...just ask me!). The reason they do not want me around is because of Who and what I represent. Believe it or not, I have heard the words, "Get out of here, preacher!" I am quite sure many other preachers have heard those words as well.

When a man gets to this level of hardness, he has all but crossed the unseen line where God is no longer going to give him the opportunity to repent. This is a dangerous place to be and no one reading these words ought to ever put himself in that position. We are told to "seek ye the LORD while he may be found, call ye upon him while he is near."[52] The implication is clear. There may come a time when God may not be found or when He is not near. That is why we must repent the moment we are under the conviction of the Holy Spirit.

Pharaoh has now arrived at that point. Moses does not argue with him nor does he try to convince him that God is right. "And Moses said, Thou hast spoken well, I will see thy face again no more" (Exodus 10:29). The ninth plague has ended with the last meeting between the prophet and the king. There would be no more confrontations, no more clashes, and no more discussions.

Pharaoh has run the table—he has defied the living God to the greatest degree. Now it was time for God to do what He promised Moses He would do in the very beginning of this narrative. I repeat it here for

---

[52] Isaiah 55:6.

emphasis sake. "And thou shalt say unto Pharaoh, Thus saith the LORD, Israel is my son, even my firstborn: And I say unto thee, Let my son go, that he may serve me: and if thou refuse to let him go, behold, I will slay thy son, even thy firstborn."[53] Pharaoh has sowed one too many seeds of rebellion and will soon pay a price he has no desire to pay.

Think about your life for a moment. Have you ever been at a point where you did not want anyone around you that reminded you of the truth of God's word? Could that be why you are not as faithful to attend church as you should? Is that why you have abandoned your Christian friends and replaced them with some acquaintances that are not so "holy?" I remember Adam and Eve hiding in the Garden of Eden because they did not want to have a face-to-face encounter with a holy God.

I urge you to not let that be your testimony. God has given you His word. He has allowed things to happen in your life to draw you to Him. That is how much He loves you. He does not want you to run away from Him. He desires for you to come to Him; so, seek Him while you have time and while He may be found! Here is a Word from God to Israel in the days of Zechariah, the prophet. I pray it will be a word of encouragement to you as I close this chapter. "Thus saith the LORD of hosts; Turn ye unto me, saith the LORD of hosts, and I will turn unto you, saith the LORD of hosts."[54] Amen!

---

[53] Exodus 4:22-23.

[54] Zechariah 1:3.

Chapter Eight: The Calm Before The Storm

And the LORD said unto Moses,
Yet will I bring one plague more upon Pharaoh,
and upon Egypt; afterwards he will let you go...
Exodus 11:1

As I write this chapter, the southeastern part of my home state, Texas, has just recently been hammered by Hurricane Harvey. The damage from this category four storm was enormous. The winds were devastatingly destructive, as usual; but then there was the rain—bountiful and overwhelming amounts of rain! Many places recorded well over thirty inches of rain. Can you imagine almost three-feet of rain falling where you live? It was indeed a storm of epic proportion.

I watched TV weathermen who, for some strange reason, volunteered to do live broadcasts during the hurricane. (I hope they got paid well!) One thing so remarkable to me happened when the eye of the hurricane passed over them. Suddenly, there was a calmness—no wind and no rain. They could look up and see a few glimmers of a beautiful blue sky. If it were not for the destruction already done by the wind and heavy rains, one might think that there had not been much of a storm at all; but this was only the calm before the storm.

Soon the fierce winds would begin to blow from another direction and the drenching rains would once again pound the locations from which these weathermen broadcasted. Sure enough, the eye passed. The hurricane continued and the damage worsened.

They eye of a hurricane is where we find Pharaoh and his people at the beginning of Exodus, chapter eleven: the calm before the storm. The king has told Moses to leave his presence and never come back; and in his stubborn mind, he probably thought that would be the end of things. He just did not realize he was dealing the Almighty God of the universe!

Now while Pharaoh's disobedience to God and the rejection of His word had produced his cold, obstinate heart of stone; something completely different was going on among his constituents. The Scriptures record that the LORD had given His people "favor in the sight of the Egyptians. Moreover the man Moses was very great in the land of Egypt, in the sight of Pharaoh's servants, and in the sight of the people" (Exodus 11:3). That is awesome!

This favor with the Egyptians had nothing to do with the greatness of Moses himself. His acceptance was because of what had happened in their land ever since Moses returned to Egypt. They knew that he had a God that was unlike anything they had ever seen before. This will be a great blessing and benefit to the Israelites when they finally get to leave the land of bondage. The Bible records that when this long-awaited exodus occurred, "they [the people of God] spoiled[55] the Egyptians" (Exodus 12:36).

Before that event transpires, there are a few other matters that need to be addressed. At the end of Exodus, chapter 10, we learned that Pharaoh was dismissing Moses from his presence with a threat of killing him if he ever saw him again. We also saw Moses' response in verse twenty-nine of that same chapter but Moses is not finished speaking to the king.

---

[55] The Hebrew word for "spoiled" here, used in the PIEL stem, means to plunder or strip. This was an intense gaining of the wealth of the Egyptians.

Sometimes, the chapter divisions in our Bible make it a little more difficult to see when a story line or conversation is being continued. I like these divisions but one must understand they are not divinely inspired. When we come to Exodus eleven, we discover a three-verse parenthesis in the middle of Moses' last words before Pharaoh. How do we know this? The text gives it away.

Exodus 11:4 continues Moses' final meeting with the king with the following words: "And Moses said…" When you come to the end of verse eight, you read that Moses "went out from Pharaoh in a great anger." Thus, the confrontation is over. Pharaoh has threatened Moses but Moses gets in the last word. It was a powerful ending to these meetings. I want to paraphrase the truths Moses spoke to his hard-hearted foe.

1. The LORD is going to show up at midnight in your land (11:4).
2. Any first-born person or animal in your land will die at that time (11:5).
3. The grief in your land is going to be greater than anything ever seen or heard in the past or in the future (11:6).
4. The dogs are not even going to bark at my people (11:7).
5. You are going to know that my God has clearly demonstrated there is a difference between your people and His people (11:7).
6. All your servants and everyone that follows you are going to bow down to me and beg me to take my people and leave Egypt (11:8).
7. After this all happens, we are leaving Egypt (11:8).

With that, Moses goes out from Pharaoh with a righteous fury. As stated on the previous page, he departs "in a great anger." The Hebrew word here for "great" is only used six times in the Old Testament. According to *Strong's Concordance*, it is translated as "fierce" (3x), "great" (2x), and "heat" (1x).[56] It is always used to define the word "anger." Therefore, we can glean that when Moses left the court of the king, he was heated with anger. Why he is this way is not stated. I am willing to accept the fact that we are not told the reason. I just know he was very angry.

With all that has been said, the stage is now set for the tenth and final plague—the death of the firstborn. Moses has now gone back to his people. He returns to them with a message. "Get your Passover lambs ready and pack your bags. We are leaving town!"[57] He has done all he can to present Jehovah God to Pharaoh. God has been rejected every single time. The king had been warned in the beginning of this story[58] and Moses reminds him in their last face-to-face encounter what was about to happen. Pharaoh's firstborn son would soon die.

Pharaoh's DISOBEYING THE WORD OF GOD has now run its course. His heart is hard. God has spoken to Moses, "Yet will I bring one plague more upon Pharaoh, and upon Egypt; afterwards he will let you go hence: when he shall let you go, he shall surely thrust you out hence

---

[56] This information is available online for free at www.blueletterbible.org. https://www.blueletterbible.org/lang/lexicon/lexicon.cfm?Strongs=H2750&t=KJV.

[57] This is just a very simple paraphrase of Exodus 12:21-28.

[58] See Exodus 3:21-23 where God tells Moses to let Pharaoh know that if he refuses to let His people go, his firstborn son would die.

altogether" (Exodus 11:1). In just a few more hours, this prideful king and his people will pay a terrible price for his stony heart; and then, he will obey God. This is the calm before the storm.

One might wonder what the king's thoughts were as he approached the midnight hour on that fateful day. Did he ever wonder if Moses' words were right? Did he believe at any moment he was going to lose his firstborn son?

When he tucked his son in at bedtime that last night, did he stay at the bedside a little longer—watching his son breathe and hoping he would still be breathing the next morning? Did he kneel beside his sleeping firstborn son and pray to his gods? (They had been totally ineffective during the season of plagues. Was Moses' God that much more powerful?) Did he check the doors of his palace a second time to make sure they were locked? Did he double the security that night or was his heart so hard he never had a single though that Moses had spoken the truth?

That is the danger of cultivating and maintaining a hard heart. You reach a point where you are no longer able to accept God's truth. You are adamantly opposed to God, the Bible, and those that call themselves Christians. You may think, "God's people are morons;" or "The Bible is way outdated and old-fashion." As for God, He is at best, a thorn in your side.

Lest you get the idea that only the heathen can develop a hard heart, I must hasten to say that even Christians can have one as well. When you consider the first step, DISOBEYING THE WORD OF GOD, that puts us all on level ground. Every one of us has, at some point,

47

disobeyed God's word; and that is where we start our journey on a path that can lead to a Pharaoh-like hard heart.

What we must do is stop the process before it gets too far—before we get to the point that we no longer respond at all to God's truth. We must repent of our disobedience and turn back to God. We must guard our hearts diligently so that we never allow those gears to keep turning. We do not want to be stubborn and stiff-necked. We want a soft and pliable heart so that God can mold us into what He wants us to be.

I hope, if you are reading this book, that you are not experiencing a calm before the storm. Pharaoh was told exactly what would happen if he refused to obey God. You probably have no clue; but, I can assure you, if you continue down that road, the price of not obeying the Lord will be much greater than you want to pay.

I close this chapter with the words of Hosea, the prophet of God. "Sow to yourselves in righteousness, reap in mercy; break up your fallow ground: *for it is time to seek the LORD…*" (Hosea 10:12) (emphasis mine).

Chapter Nine: The Midnight Storm
And Moses said, Thus saith the LORD,
About midnight will I go out into the midst of Egypt.
Exodus 11:4

There is a time in the daylight hours in which, in a sense, marks the halfway part of the day. We call this point high-noon. It is when the sun stands directly over your head. When that occurs, you have no shadow. You are enveloped totally in the sunlight and there is no darkness. Just writing this opening paragraph makes me want to go outside at noon and test this out. Have you ever considered what would be the opposite of high-noon?

Would it not be midnight? In using the same idea to describe high-noon, midnight, the halfway part of the night, would be the time at which everything is in darkness. You are engulfed completely in darkness and there is no light. Since the word of God declares that "God is light, and in him is no darkness at all,"[59] we are not surprised that the midnight hour is, at times, associated with the occult.[60]

However, there are some interesting things recorded in the Bible that happened at midnight. Samson, in the Book of Judges, to escape the Gazites who were plotting to kill him, did an amazing thing at midnight. "And Samson lay till midnight, and arose at midnight, and took the doors of the gate of the city, and the two posts, and went away with them, bar

---

[59] I John 1:5.

[60] The witching hour is a time of night when supernatural creatures are believed to be particularly active, making it a prime time of night for witchcraft. Many people think of midnight specifically as the witching hour, while others more generally associate it with the dead of night, the dark hours when few people are awake and about. Taken from www.answers.com/Q/What_is_the_witching_hour.

and all, and put them upon his shoulders, and carried them up to the top of an hill that is before Hebron."[61] Paul and Silas found themselves in the city of Philippi in a prison; and at the midnight hour, they burst out with singing. "And at midnight Paul and Silas prayed, and sang praises unto God: and the prisoners heard them. And suddenly there was a great earthquake, so that the foundations of the prison were shaken: and immediately all the doors were opened, and every one's bands were loosed."[62] The Philippian jailer will be eternally grateful for that midnight event for he and is family received Jesus Christ as their Lord and Savior before sunrise as a result of God's miraculous manifestation.

As we get back to the Exodus story, Pharaoh is going to have a midnight experience; but his late-night appointment will not be a good one for him or his people. The calm is just about over, a powerful midnight storm is coming, and it will be a total disaster for the hard-hearted King of Egypt. Payday has come. He will now suffer for all of his disobedience to the holy God of Israel.

Moses and the people of Israel had already received instructions from God on what to do. They would be ready for the midnight disaster. A new day had come for them. Before the Law of Moses was ever written, God established a celebration for them called Passover. You can read about their Passover preparations in Exodus 12:1-20. Here is a condensed version of these verses.

1. Select a young lamb, without spot or blemish, for a sacrifice.

---

[61] This story is recorded in Judges 16:1-3.

[62] This great event is recorded in Acts 16:16-40.

2. When you kill this lamb, take the shed blood and sprinkle it on your door posts.

3. When you eat the lamb, make sure you are fully dressed and ready to move out.

4. Remember this is the Lord's Passover.

5. The Lord is going to pass through the land tonight and slay the firstborn of man and beast in Egypt.

6. When I see the blood on the door posts, I will pass over your home and your firstborn will be safe.

7. Don't forget to celebrate this feast through all your generations.

Those were the basic guidelines Moses presented to his people. Now the Hebrew people were to wait for the fourteenth day of this beginning of months[63] to execute God's commands.

When Moses left Pharaoh's court for the last time, he had told him that on midnight of that day, "all the firstborn in the land of Egypt shall die" (Exodus 11:5). The date must have been the 14th day of the new month because Moses, after he left the king's presence, went back to his people and issued the following command: "Draw out and take you a lamb according to your families, and kill the passover. And ye shall take a bunch of hyssop, and dip it in the blood that is in the bason, and strike the lintel and the two side posts with the blood that is in the bason; and none of you shall go out at the door of his house until the morning. For the LORD will pass through to smite the Egyptians; and when he seeth the

---

[63] See Exodus 12:2-6. The lamb could not be chosen until the 10th day of the new month. It could not be sacrificed until the 14th day of the month.

blood upon the lintel, and on the two side posts, the LORD will pass over the door, and will not suffer the destroyer to come in unto your houses to smite you" (Exodus 12:21-23).

The Israelites would be safe if they would simply obey the Lord. The good news is that they did! "And the children of Israel went away, and did as the LORD had commanded Moses and Aaron, so did they" (Exodus 12:28).

Meanwhile, back in Pharaoh's palace and with his people, no such preparations were being made. I can picture in my mind some of his servants coming to him and telling him about the bloodbath taking place in the land of Goshen. "Have you heard what those crazy Israelites are doing? They are slaughtering their own lambs by the hundreds! What in the name of our gods are they doing?" (Actually, it wasn't in the name of the Egyptians' gods at all!) Perhaps Pharaoh laughed and scoffed along with them at the supposed foolishness of Moses and his people; but maybe, just maybe, there was a tiny hint of apprehension in his mind. After all, there had never been this kind of activity by his captors before this day. What were they up to? Little did he know that the midnight storm was only a few short hours away.

The daylight hours disappeared and nightfall came. The people of God were inside their homes. They had enjoyed their Passover meal; and now they sat waiting, fully dressed, but waiting. Perhaps some of them were wondering if they had done enough or had put the blood on the door posts the right way. Would the shed blood of an innocent lamb be enough to save them? Sleep could not have come too easily. They may have even kept their firstborn child as close to them as they could. Would their trust in God keep their loved one safe?

Among the Egyptians, night life went on as usual. Only Pharaoh had been told about the midnight death threat. If he shared this perilous news with his people, we have no record. Most of the families went to bed that night with no clue as to what was going to happen long before they would normally awaken. Only the king himself knew about the possibility of a massive plague of death to strike every home in his kingdom at the midnight hour.

And then the clock struck midnight. "And it came to pass, that at midnight the LORD smote all the firstborn in the land of Egypt, from the firstborn of Pharaoh that sat on his throne unto the firstborn of the captive that was in the dungeon; and all the firstborn of cattle" (Exodus 12:29). Suddenly and quickly, the Lord[64] had swept through Egypt leaving every home with the bitter taste of death. Only among the Israelites, under the banner of the blood of the Passover lamb, was everyone safe. Just like God had told the Egyptian king through Moses, he was going to know "that the LORD doth put a difference between the Egyptians and Israel" (Exodus 11:7).

"And Pharaoh rose up in the night, he, and all his servants, and all the Egyptians; and there was a great cry in Egypt; for there was not a house where there was not one dead" (Exodus 12:30). God had mentioned this wailing too. "And there shall be a great cry throughout all the land of

---

[64] Even though many speak of a death angel slaying the firstborn in Egypt, it is clear that the LORD does this Himself.

Egypt, such as there was none like it, nor shall be like it any more" (Exodus 11:6).

The scene before us is unimaginable. There was gut-wrenching, heart-breaking sorrow throughout all of Egypt; and all because of one man who refused to obey God. The midnight storm had come and the man who had hardened his heart toward the God of heaven is now facing the most difficult situation his family and his kingdom have ever faced. Death has gripped every nook and corner of the land he so proudly ruled. Pharaoh and his people have paid a heavy price for his obstinate heart.

I hope you can see now why it is so important to make sure you guard your heart as the Bible records in Proverbs 4:23: "Keep thy heart with all diligence; for out of it are the issues of life." You never want to go as far as Pharaoh went. You want to stop this process long before God's judgment falls and you reap the sowing of the seed of disobedience and rebellion against Him.

You are the only one that can stop the turning of the gears. I love how the psalmist referred to this repentance. Hear what he said and make this your decision while you still can. "I thought on my ways, and turned my feet unto thy testimonies. I made haste, and delayed not to keep thy commandments."[65]

---

[65] Psalm 119:59-60.

Chapter Ten: Free At Last

And he called for Moses and Aaron by night, and said,
Rise up, and get you forth from among my people,
both ye and the children of Israel;
and go, serve the LORD, as ye have said.
Exodus 12:31

On August 28, 1963, Martin Luther King Jr. stood on the steps of the Lincoln Memorial in Washington, D. C., and made his infamous *I Have A Dream* speech. His speech ends with these well-known words. "Free at last! free at last! thank God Almighty, we are free at last!"[66] Over three thousand years before that discourse was spoken, the people of God, Israel, led by Moses and Aaron had their own "Free at last" song to sing. It came after over 400 years of bondage to the taskmasters and pharaohs of Egypt, happening just like God had prophesied.

The actual exodus or departure from Egypt does not take long to tell, encompassing only a few verses in the biblical account.[67] It took place rather rapidly. Pharaoh finally realized he had lost to Moses and his God. His son had died and every home in his kingdom had death also knock on its door. This was the proverbial "straw that broke the camel's back."

Exodus 12:31-32 records, "And he called for Moses and Aaron by night, and said, Rise up, and get you forth from among my people, both ye and the children of Israel; and go, serve the LORD, as ye have said. Also take your flocks and your herds, as ye have said, and be gone; and bless

---

[66] Copied from text of Dr. King's full speech found at https://www.usconstitution.net/dream.html.

[67] Exodus 12:31-41 sums up this part of the Exodus account

55

me also."[68] Notice that the king did not wait until sunrise to dismiss the Israelites. The nighttime had not passed, but he was wide awake; and apparently, his people were as well. They joined in the movement to rid their land of these troublesome people. "And the Egyptians were urgent upon the people, that they might send them out of the land in haste; for they said, We be all dead men" (Exodus 12:33).

I recall that the Lord, through Moses, had mentioned this action of the king's citizens a little earlier in our story. Remember what Moses told Pharaoh in their final meeting? "And all these thy servants shall come down unto me, and bow down themselves unto me, saying, Get thee out, and all the people that follow thee: and after that I will go out" (Exodus 11:8). Just like the Lord had stated, the people were urging and even begging the Israelites to leave.

Can you hear the sense of urgency in their voices? These people were not acting in faith, they were acting out of fear. They were afraid they might be next on the list to die. They thought their only way of dealing with this was to rid their homeland of Moses and his people. Repentance never entered their mind. It is no wonder the Scriptures record in Exodus 11:1 that when it came time for the people of God to leave their land of bondage, they would be "thrust" out "altogether." The New Living Translation reads in this manner: "He [the king] will be so eager to get rid of you that he will force you all to leave."

That is exactly what happened here. The Hebrew word for "thrust" means to drive away, drive out, or expel. When you add the fact that this

---

[68] It is interesting to note that Pharaoh wanted a blessing. It is also equally interesting to note that no response from Moses was recorded. It could be that Pharaoh's heart was so hardened that he was no longer in a position to be blessed by God.

word was written using the PIEL stem,[69] you understand that this was a strong, forceful compelling of the Hebrew children to get out of Egypt ASAP and doing it with haste![70] That would be no problem for God's people. They had wanted to leave for a long, long time; and in fact, Moses had told them to eat the Passover "with your loins girded, your shoes on your feet, and your staff in your hand; and ye shall eat it in haste: it is the LORD'S Passover" (Exodus 12:11). He knew they were leaving the country shortly after midnight—not long after they had celebrated Passover; and they were fully dressed and ready to go!

By the way, there is one more thing God got right about this! Way back in the third chapter of Exodus, before Moses ever confronted Pharaoh, the Lord gave him a promise. "And I will give this people favor in the sight of the Egyptians: and it shall come to pass, that, when ye go, ye shall not go empty: but every woman shall borrow of her neighbor, and of her that sojourneth in her house, jewels of silver, and jewels of gold, and raiment: and ye shall put them upon your sons, and upon your daughters; and ye shall spoil the Egyptians."[71]

Just like the God of Israel said, it happened. "And the children of Israel did according to the word of Moses; and they borrowed of the Egyptians jewels of silver, and jewels of gold, and raiment: and the LORD gave the people favor in the sight of the Egyptians, so that they lent unto them such things as they required. And they spoiled the Egyptians"

---

[69] See page 8, the first full paragraph, for a description of a PIEL stem verb.

[70] See Exodus 12:33 where it says that the Egyptians sent the Hebrews "out of the land in haste."

[71] Exodus 3:21-22.

(Exodus 12:35-36). You have to love that! This is what you call meeting their needs in abundance!

We read these words. "Now the sojourning of the children of Israel, who dwelt in Egypt, was four hundred and thirty years. And it came to pass at the end of the four hundred and thirty years, even the selfsame day it came to pass, that all the hosts of the LORD went out from the land of Egypt" (Exodus 12:40-41). I can hear them singing, ""Free at last! free at last! thank God Almighty, we are free at last!"

You might think this is a good place to end this story and to finish this book, but God is not through with Pharaoh yet. You see, having a hard heart toward God is costly. You do not want one. Sure, the king has lost his firstborn son and his kingdom has suffered greatly, but he still has a heart of stone; and believe it or not, the hard-heartening gears have one last turn in them before there is nothing left to harden of Pharaoh's heart. The Scriptures warn us, "It is a fearful thing to fall into the hands of the living God."[72] I pray that you will repent before you ever experience this aspect of Almighty God.

---

[72] Hebrews 10:31.

Chapter Eleven: Pharaoh's Last Stand

And Moses said unto the people, Fear ye not, stand still,
and see the salvation of the LORD,
which he will shew to you today:
for the Egyptians whom ye have seen today,
ye shall see them again no more forever.
Exodus 14:13

Have you ever heard of Custer's Last Stand? This epic clash took place at the Battle of Little Big Horn in Montana on June 25, 1876. "General George Armstrong Custer [was] a daring, dashing, impetuous soldier, who had won high honors as a division commander during the Civil War, and who had developed a reputation as an Indian Fighter when he led his gallant regiment against the Kiowas and the Cheyennes on the Southern plains."[73] However, this impetuous spirit led to his defeat.

Instead of obeying the commands of his superiors, he rushed ahead into a battle against a tribe of Indians he thought was running from the battle. Instead, they were arming for the battle. On that fateful day, General Custer was killed along with a large part of his battalion. Had he waited just one day, the outcome surely would have been different. Reinforcements were on the way. One report of General Custer tells us that he was "savoring the chance to have all the Glory to himself."[74] The subheading of the article from which this quote comes labels this part of the Little Big Horn battle, "Pride Comes Before The Fall."[75]

---

[73] Taken from *Custer's Last Stand*, http://www.sonofthesouth.net/union-generals/custer/custers-last-stand.htm.

[74] Ibid.

[75] Ibid.

Pride comes before the fall—sounds a lot like Pharaoh. In this chapter, we will discover his personal "last stand." It all started when he freed the Israelites. They had left Egypt but God sovereignly directed their departure path a little differently than might have been expected. "And it came to pass, when Pharaoh had let the people go, that God led them not through the way of the land of the Philistines, although that was near…but God led the people about, through the way of the wilderness of the Red sea…" Since we are familiar with the story, we know what is going to happen at the Red Sea; but I find it quite interesting to learn that God is the One setting the scenario up for Pharaoh's Last Stand!

By the time they arrive at the banks of the sea, they are going to be between the legendary "rock and a hard place." Why would God allow this to happen? The Israelites are trapped (or so it seems); but God has a plan—He always does! He tells Moses that Pharaoh is going to say, "They are entangled in the land, the wilderness hath shut them in" (Exodus 14:3). When that happens, the Lord lets his servant know that He "will harden Pharaoh's heart, that he shall follow after them; and I will be honored upon Pharaoh, and upon all his host; that the Egyptians may know that I am the LORD" (14:4).

Sure enough, this is exactly what happened. The King of Egypt was told what was going on and the Scriptures record that "the heart[76] of Pharaoh and of his servants was turned against the people, and they said, Why have we done this, that we have let Israel go from serving us? And he made ready his chariot, and took his people with him" (14:5-6). Not only did the king do what was prophesied, God did what He proclaimed

---

[76] Once again, we see that Pharaoh's heart is the culprit.

He would do. "And the LORD hardened the heart of Pharaoh king of Egypt, and he pursued after the children of Israel…" (14:8).

There apparently was a tiny spot in Pharaoh's heart that had not been turned to stone. Now the process is coming to an absolute and irrevocable finish. There is no room or time for repentance. The Egyptian king has crossed the point of no return. He is going to make one last stand against God's people; but make no mistake about it, this will be his final one. His prideful and hard heart has brought him to a place for his complete demise.

We know what is about to take place. Pharaoh and his army march quickly and fervently to catch up with Moses and his people. When they get them in their sights, they see that the Israelites are cornered. The children of God are facing the Red Sea on one front and their angry enemy on the other. A spirit of panic begins to take over the hearts of those that were, only three short days ago, singing and shouting about their freedom.

They express their fears to Moses but they do not sway him. He stays strong in his faith. "And Moses said unto the people, Fear ye not, stand still, and see the salvation of the LORD, which he will shew to you today: for the Egyptians whom ye have seen today, ye shall see them again no more forever. The LORD shall fight for you, and ye shall hold your peace" (Exodus 14:13-14). (I love it when God fights for us. We win every time!)

God tells Moses to stretch out his rod over the Red Sea; and when he would do this, God would then divide the waters and allow His children to walk through the middle of that sea on dry ground.[77] Then one last

---

[77] Exodus 14:16.

time, God declares that what He is going to do; and this time, it is not just the king who will experience the hardening of the heart! "And I, behold, I will harden the hearts of the Egyptians, and they shall follow them: and I will get me honor upon Pharaoh, and upon all his host, upon his chariots, and upon his horsemen. And the Egyptians shall know that I am the LORD, when I have gotten me honor upon Pharaoh, upon his chariots, and upon his horsemen" (Exodus 14:17-18).

The Lord lets us in on a biblical truth here that we need to remember. Too many people think that they can sin and not affect anyone else. I have heard this said often through the years, "I'm not hurting anyone but me." That is such a lie of the devil. Sin contaminates— spreads like a virus—rages like a wildfire. You cannot sin and isolate yourself from its widespread consequences. Sin will bring you down but it will also take others down with you. Ask Adam. Ask Achan. Ask King David.

Pharaoh's rejection of God and his disobedience to the word of God has infected his people now. They are just as hard-hearted as he. They, who once held Moses in great esteem,[78] have now willingly joined forces with their king to chase the Israelites down and do whatever it would take to bring them once again into bondage. Thankfully, God would have not part of their wicked schemes.

While God held the pursuing army back with His miraculous cloud of darkness,[79] the children of Israel walked across the Red Sea on dry

---

[78] See Exodus 11:3 where we are told that "Moses was very great in the land of Egypt..."

[79] Exodus 14:19-20.

ground. We read that "and the waters were a wall unto them on their right hand, and on their left" (Exodus 14:22). What a crossing that must have been! The Egyptian army must have thought that anything the Israelites could do, they could do better. We read that they "pursued, and went in after them to the midst of the sea, even all Pharaoh's horses, his chariots, and his horsemen" (Exodus 14:23).

What happened next, as most of you well know, is the last piece of evidence of the judgment of God on the hard-hearted Pharaoh and his people. I remind us all again of Proverbs 29:1. "He, that being often reproved hardeneth his neck, shall suddenly be destroyed, and that without remedy." The King of Egypt had been often reproved but he had refused to obey God. His destruction would be swift and certain. There was no remedy now for his heart disease.

Let's read the rest of the story without any commentary or remarks along the way.

"And it came to pass, that in the morning watch the LORD looked unto the host of the Egyptians through the pillar of fire and of the cloud, and troubled the host of the Egyptians, and took off their chariot wheels, that they drave them heavily: so that the Egyptians said, Let us flee from the face of Israel; for the LORD fighteth for them against the Egyptians. And the LORD said unto Moses, Stretch out thine hand over the sea, that the waters may come again upon the Egyptians, upon their chariots, and upon their horsemen. And Moses stretched forth his hand over the sea, and the sea returned to his strength when the morning appeared; and the Egyptians fled against it; and the LORD overthrew the Egyptians in the midst of the sea. And the waters returned, and covered the chariots, and the horsemen, and all the host of Pharaoh that came into the sea after them; there remained not so much as one of them. But the children of Israel walked upon dry land in the midst of the sea; and the waters were a wall unto them on their right hand, and on their left. Thus the LORD saved Israel that day out of the hand of the Egyptians; and Israel saw the Egyptians dead upon the sea shore. And Israel saw that great work which the LORD did upon the Egyptians: and the people feared the LORD, and believed the LORD, and his servant Moses" (Exodus 14:24-31).

The battle is all over now. The Israelites are completely free. The Egyptians have lost their army—not one of them survived. There is some debate on whether Pharaoh perished with his men. We know from Exodus 14:6-7 that he got his chariot and his men ready. It is evident that he headed out with his army to chase Moses for verse eight tells us "he pursued after the children of Israel." When you read verse ten, we learn "Pharaoh drew nigh" to the Israelites. There is no doubt from the word of God that he is present at the Red Sea.

When you consider Pharaoh's total disrespect for God, Moses, and Israel, there is no reason to think that he would have not led his own army to track down those that he hated so much. After all, had they not been the cause of the death of his son? If he could have the opportunity for revenge, would he not actively seek retribution? It seemed like not only a possibility but a probability that he could make this happen especially when he saw his enemy being trapped by the Red Sea.

I believe he died on that day; but honestly, it is really a moot point. He and his kingdom suffered such a devastating defeat that all life was drained out of him. His defiance of the God of heaven had backfired. If he did survive, there was no more power left in his punch—no fire in his spirit—no joy in his soul. That is what a hard heart will get you— absolutely nothing!

After getting this far in this book, I pray that you are not following the way of Pharaoh. Rejecting the Lord will get you nowhere and get you there quickly. Stop where you are right now and turn back to God! Repent before you cross that unseen "point of no return."

Hebrews 3:15 issues this plea: "While it is said, Today if ye will hear his voice, harden not your hearts…" I echo these words and beg you to not harden your heart! Turn back to Jesus today!

Chapter Twelve: A Final Word

But after thy hardness and impenitent heart
treasurest up unto thyself wrath
against the day of wrath and revelation
of the righteous judgment of God.
Romans 2:5

I have been a pastor for almost thirty-six years. I have heard hundreds of sermons in my life time (most of them pretty good) and preached well over four thousand messages myself (most of them pretty good—I hope!). I have been to Bible college and Seminary. There is one principle about sin I have heard repeated by many preachers and have found written in several commentaries. It concerns the terrible fall of Samson, recorded in the Book of Judges, due to his sin. Perhaps you have heard this truth too. "Sin will take you further than you want to go, keep you longer than you want to stay, and cost you more than you want to pay." (I really do not know who first said this; and so, I cannot give credit where credit is due!)

That is what happened to Pharaoh and his people. That is what will happen to any person who continues to disobey God and develop a hard heart. The verse below the title of this chapter declares it well. A person that refuses to repent and hardens his heart is not earning God's favor and blessings. The Revised Standard Version says it like this. "But by your hard and impenitent heart you are storing up wrath for yourself on the day of wrath when God's righteous judgment will be revealed." I must admit that storing up the wrath of God to be poured out on me in judgment is not on my "to do" list.

Why would anyone want to do that anyway; and yet, we know it happens. The Scriptures show us the heart of God concerning man. He is "is longsuffering to us-ward, not willing that any should perish, but that all should come to repentance."[80] That has always been his desire—He wants man to repent. Paul described this heart of our Lord by telling young Timothy that God "will have all men to be saved, and to come unto the knowledge of the truth."[81] Is not this one of the great messages of John 3:16? This being the case, man has to totally disregard the God of the Bible in order to NOT know the truth.

That was Pharaoh's approach to God. It started the day he DISOBEYED THE WORD OF GOD, but he did not stop there. He DENIED THE WORK OF GOD, DISTORTED THE WAY OF GOD, DISCOUNTED THE WISDOM OF GOD, DEFIED THE WORTH OF GOD, and finally, DISAVOWED THE WORKER OF GOD. Each step along the way, his heart got a little harder toward God. The gears turned and turned until there was nothing left to turn. Pharaoh went too far— crossed that point of no return. God gave him ample time to repent and demonstrated His greatness and superiority, but the king rejected Him every time. God offered grace but the king refused to receive it.

When man stubbornly refuses to bow to the one and only true God and will not humble himself under His "mighty hand,"[82] he leaves a holy and righteous God no choice but to bring judgment. Yes, God is patient and longsuffering; but He is bound by His word to bring that judgment.

---

[80] 2 Peter 3:9.

[81] I Timothy 2:4.

[82] See I Peter 5:6.

When man has completely filled up his storage container of wrath because of a hard heart and an unrepentant spirit, the time comes for that wrath to be poured out. This happens time and time again in the Bible. Pharaoh is just one of the greatest examples of this. (The Book of Revelation speaks of a future time when this will happen worldwide.)

So, the time has come for you, the reader, to do one last evaluation of your heart. Be careful here—remember your heart is "deceitful above all things, and desperately wicked."[83] Would you say that your heart is fully devoted to God? God wants that. He deserves that. Here is what King Asa found out about this. "For the eyes of the LORD run to and fro throughout the whole earth, to shew himself strong in the behalf of them whose heart is perfect toward him..."[84]

God wants to demonstrate to someone on this earth just how strong and powerful He is! That is so neat! He would have done that for Pharaoh but the king would have nothing to do with Him. He would love to do it for you, but it is truly a matter of your heart. How is your heart today? Are you walking in disobedience to Him and allowing those gears to turn that will one day harden your heart unless you repent? Stop where you are in your life now, while you have time! Turn back to the Lord.

Hear these words from the Lord: "He that covereth his sins shall not prosper: but whoso confesseth and forsaketh them shall have mercy."[85]

---

[83] Jeremiah 17:9.

[84] 2 Chronicles 16:9.

[85] Proverbs 28:13.

"If we confess our sins, he is faithful and just to forgive us our sins, and to cleanse us from all unrighteousness."[86]

I have one last thought to share with you and to encourage you. The words below come from a song—one that you are may know. We sing this song in our church from time to time. It is a great song about the heart. The song is *Change My Heart Oh God* and was written by Eddie Espinosa.[87] May this be your prayer as you strive to "trust in the LORD with all thine heart; and lean not unto thine own understanding."[88]

> Change my heart Oh God, make it ever true.
> Change my heart Oh God, may I be like You.
> You are the potter, I am the clay,
> Mold me and make me, this is what I pray.
> Change my heart Oh God, make it ever true.
> Change my heart Oh God, may I be like You.

Amen and amen!

---

[86] I John 1:9.

[87] 1982 Mercy / Vineyard Publishing (Admin. by Vineyard Music USA).

[88] Proverbs 3:5.

Appendix 1: The Steps to Hardening Your Heart

1. Disobey the Word of God—Chapter 2

2. Deny the Work of God—Chapter 3

3. Distort the Way of God—Chapter 4

4. Discount the Wisdom of God—Chapter 5

5. Defy the Worth of God—Chapter 6

6. Disavow the Worker of God—Chapter 7

Appendix 2: Repentance and Salvation

I have used a word throughout this paper that is essential to our eternity that I want to address in this appendix. It is the word "repent." It basically means to have a change of mind (heart) that results in a change of direction in a person's life. We observed the life of Pharaoh in this book and discovered that he never did repent. Instead, he kept on hardening his heart toward God which led to his ultimate downfall.

His life perfectly illustrates the words of Jesus in Luke 13:3. "Except ye repent, ye shall all likewise perish." That is a serious statement. Repentance is the key to salvation; and so, I want to take a few moments to share with you God's simple plan of salvation.

It starts with recognizing that we are a sinner. That should be easy because we all stand on equal ground at this point. The Scriptures point out that "all have sinned, and come short of the glory of God."[89] God's commandments have been broken. We are guilty; and because of this, we are under the condemnation of death—we are destined to perish.

"The wages of sin is death; but the gift of God is eternal life through Jesus Christ our Lord."[90] Praise God that He has provided a gift for us—one that cancels the debt we owe and gives us eternal life! This is God's free gift. That is indeed good news; which is the definition of the word, gospel. In writing about this gospel, the Apostle Paul tells us "that

---

[89] Romans 3:23.

[90] Romans 6:23.

71

Christ died for our sins according to the scriptures."[91] That means that when Jesus died on the cross, He was dying in our place—paying the wages of our sins; but we must remember that this is a gift.

In order for a gift to do me any good, I have to receive the gift and open it up. If I leave the gift on a table and walk away, I gain no benefit from it. That is the same thing with this wonderful gift from God. John 3:16 expounds on this. "For God so loved the world, that he gave his only begotten Son, that whosoever believeth in him should not perish, but have everlasting life." The gift of God was His son, Jesus, dying on the cross of Calvary and it was given to us in love[92]; but again, we have to take this gift and make it our own.

Why do I need this gift? That is simple. If I reject this gift of love from God, I will perish. That means I will die as an unforgiven sinner and will spend eternity in hell. If I refuse to turn from my sin and turn to Jesus (this is repentance), I condemn myself to that kind of eternity. Just like Pharaoh continually rejected God and ended up perishing in the Red Sea, I am headed down an eternal road of death if I choose not to repent.

On one occasion, Paul was speaking to a group of elders. He told them about the message he had been preaching. It was easy to understand: "repentance toward God, and faith toward our Lord Jesus Christ."[93] That sums up the gospel message. You must turn to God and place your faith

---

[91] I Corinthians 15:3.

[92] Romans 5:8 tells us that God demonstrated His great love to us "while we were yet sinners."

[93] Acts 20:21.

72

in the Lord Jesus Christ. After all, He is the One that died for you and is the only One that can save you.

Paul gave us a definitive word on salvation in Romans 10:9-10. "That if thou shalt confess with thy mouth the Lord Jesus, and shalt believe in thine heart that God hath raised him from the dead, thou shalt be saved. For with the heart man believeth unto righteousness; and with the mouth confession is made unto salvation." (There is that word "heart" again!) You, of course, would not believe that Jesus rose from the dead unless you first believed that He died on the cross. Paul makes one more statement that gives us a final piece of the puzzle. He writes in Romans 10:13 these important words. "For whosoever shall call upon the name of the Lord shall be saved."

So, there you have it. Jesus loved you so much that He died on the cross to pay the price of death for your sins. Just as the Passover lamb's blood was put on the door posts of the Israelites' homes and protected them from the judgment of death the night God's judgment fell on Egypt, the blood of Jesus, God's perfect Lamb, was shed at Calvary to save anyone who would turn to Him from the eternal death he deserves because he is a sinner. That indeed is good news.

How about it? Have you ever repented—turned from your sins and placed your faith in the Lord Jesus Christ? If not, I want to give you the opportunity right now, as you are reading this, to do so. Admit to God you are a sinner and have broken His commandments. Tell Him you are sorry for your sins and you know you deserve to die and go to hell. Let Him know you believe He died on the cross for you and He rose from the

73

dead. Confess you are willing to turn from your sins and your way of life and you want to turn to Him, making Him the Lord of your life. Thank Him for His gift of eternal life. Thank Him for hearing your prayer and saving you!

My friend, it really is that simple; but you must be willing to repent and turn to the Lord in faith. God will not force Himself on you. He may try to get your attention; but if you continue to harden your heart toward Him, you will seal your own eternal doom. You will perish.

Please do not do that. God loves you and wants you to have a personal and loving relationship with Him. Allow Him to soften your heart. Stop those heart-hardening gears turning today! Put yourself in a position to be blessed by God!

Quoting the Apostle Paul again, he penned these words in 2 Corinthians 6:2: "Behold, now is the accepted time; behold, now is the day of salvation." Good advice. Don't delay. Turn to the Lord today while you still have time!

One more thing, if this book has touched your heart and/or if you made a new commitment of your life to Jesus because of what you have read, I would love to hear from you. You can email me at calvarypreacher@hotmail.com.

Appendix 3: Sermon Notes

These are some notes from a couple of sermons I preached in my church in preparation for the series of messages on hardening the heart. If they can be a benefit to someone, praise the Lord!

THE HEART OF THE MATTER
Ezekiel 36:22-28

The context of this passage is one that deals with the coming "rebirth" of God's people, the Jews, in the last days. The chapter that follows is the infamous chapter on the "dry bones." One day, and it appears to be very soon, the nation of Israel will have a spiritual awakening. This is prophesied throughout the Scriptures and shall surely come to pass. However, God made it known through Ezekiel that Israel, because of idolatry, ungodliness, and other sins, had profaned His name. He also points out that the only way this could be changed was for Israel to be given a "new heart."

This principle holds true for us today. It is only through having a new heart that we can be born again and live for Christ. That truly is the "Heart of the Matter."

A new heart also will I give you, and a new spirit will I put within you:
and I will take away the stony heart out of your flesh,
And I will put my spirit within you,
and cause you to walk in my statutes,
and ye shall keep my judgments, and do them.
and I will give you a heart of flesh.
Ezekiel 36:26-27

There are over 60 references in the Book of Jeremiah to the heart. God gave Jeremiah some insight and discernment to see beyond the outward impressiveness of man's religion and focus on the important condition of the heart. In the physical world, a man can look o.k. on the outside but have a bad heart. The medical world encourages us to keep a watch on things that would lead to heart trouble. In fact, regular checkups are promoted, especially if there is a history of heart disease in your family. Why? Neglecting our physical heart condition could be fatal.

The bad news spiritually is this: there is an ongoing and well-documented history of spiritual heart disease in the family of man. *"The heart is deceitful above all things and desperately wicked: who can know it"* (Jer. 17:9)? Too many people never have a spiritual checkup. Neglecting our spiritual heart condition should be of great concern to us. If we do nothing about our spiritual heart disease, we are headed for destruction. Let's take a look at some of Jeremiah's verses on the heart.

- 3:10 *Judah hath not turned unto me with her whole heart, but feignedly*
- 4:14 *O Jerusalem, wash thine heart from wickedness*
- 5:23 *This people hath a revolting and a rebellious heart*
- 7:24 *They hearkened not...but walked in the counsels and in the imagination of their evil heart, and went backward, and not forward.*
- 9:26 *All the house of Israel are uncircumcised in the heart.*
- 14:14 *The prophets prophesy lies in my name: I sent them not, neither have I commanded them...they prophesy unto you...the deceit of their heart*
- 17:10 *I the Lord search the heart, I try the reins, even to give every man according to his ways.*

Jesus picked up on this theme in the New Testament. He also refused to be impressed with the religious activity of groups like the Pharisees. Listen to His words, quoted from Isaiah:

> *This people draweth nigh unto me with their mouth,*
> *and honoreth me with their lips;*
> *but their heart is far from me. But in vain they do worship me,*
> *teaching for doctrines the commandments of men.*
> Matthew 15:8-9

Jesus goes on to say in this same chapter...

> *But those things which proceed out of the mouth come forth*
> *rom the heart;and they defile the man.*
> *For out of the heart proceed evil thoughts,*
> *murders, adulteries, fornications, thefts,*
> *false witness, blasphemies:* (18-19)

Jeremiah's solution for Israel's heart condition was to get a new heart which could only come from God.

- 24:7 *I will give them a heart to know me, that I am the Lord...they shall return to me with their whole heart.*
- 32:39 *I will give them one heart, and one way, that they may fear me forever, for the good of them, and of their children after them.*

Let's examine a few more Scriptures...

- Jeremiah 29:1 *And ye shall seek me, and find me, when ye shall search for me with all your heart.*
- Psalm 51:17 *The sacrifices of God are a broken spirit: a broken and a contrite heart, O God, thou wilt not despise.*
- 2 Chronicles 16:9 *For the eyes of the LORD run to and fro throughout the whole earth, to show himself strong in the behalf of them whose heart is perfect toward him. Herein thou hast done foolishly: therefore from henceforth thou shalt have wars.*
- Psalm 139:23-24 *Search me, O God, and know my heart: try me, and know my thoughts: And see if there be any wicked way in me, and lead me in the way everlasting.*

1. **The Implication of a Bad Heart**
   - Not specifically stated but certainly implied
   - No need of a new heart if the old one is working well
   - The heart removed is called a "stony heart"
     - Stubbornness
     - Self-willed and self-ruling
     - Certain lack of compassion—not tender
     - Cold and indifferent
     - Not pliable—set in its ways
     - Hard-hearted—unmovable—and thought to be unreachable
     - Has no desire for spiritual matters
     - Needs to be replaced
     - Not only does not obey God, it cannot obey God!
       - The nation of Israel, time and time again, proved that they had a serious heart condition. They simply would not follow God regardless of what happened. They suffered oppression after oppression, war after war, defeat after defeat, and persecution beyond belief but proved throughout history that they did not have a heart for God. They rebelled against God and served idols. They continually faced God's judgment and never were the people God wanted them to be.
       - The only way they would ever come to a point in their lives that they would fully follow God and His word would be if He supernaturally intervened and gave them a spiritual heart transplant!
       - That same truth applies to us as well.
         - Romans 3:11 There is none that understandeth, there is none that seeketh after God.

- Jeremiah 17:9 The heart is deceitful above all things, and desperately wicked: who can know it?
- Romans 7:18 For I know that in me (that is, in my flesh,) dwelleth no good thing.

- **Man's greatest need is for a new heart!**
  - This is not a renovation, makeover, upgrade, or being refurbished.
  - Man does not have a virus that needs to be cured—he has a fatal heart disease.
  - The only cure is a total heart replacement

2. **The Insertion of a New Heart**
   - It is beyond my capability to do this for myself.
   - It is totally and completely a work of God (notice the "I will's).
   - It is a heart of flesh.
     - Soft and pliable
     - Not stubborn and therefore willing to submit
     - Warm and tender
     - Everything the stony heart was not, this new heart is!

3. **The Indications of a New Heart**
   - Comes with a new spirit or new life
     - John 6:63 *It is the spirit that quickeneth; the flesh profiteth nothing: the words that I speak unto you, they are spirit, and they are life.*
     - 2 Corinthians 3:17 *Now the Lord is that Spirit: and where the Spirit of the Lord is, there is liberty.*
   - Comes with a new ownership—the Lord lives in us through His Spirit
     - 1 Corinthians 6:19-20 *What? know ye not that your body is the temple of the Holy Ghost which is in you, which ye have of God, and ye are not your own? For ye are bought with a price: therefore glorify God in your body, and in your spirit, which are God's.*

- Comes with a new desire: you will walk with God and keep His commandments
- Comes with a changed life (no longer a stony heart but a heart of flesh)
- Comes with a new relationship: God becomes Your God—a personal relationship with a holy God
- Comes with new and greater blessings (see Ezek. 36:29-30)
- 2 Cor. 5:17 *Therefore if any man be in Christ, he is a new creature: old things are passed away; behold, all things are become new.*

About The Author

Dr. Robert (Bobby) Roger was born in Big Spring, Texas and is a graduate of Big Spring High School. He attended Howard County Junior College there for three semesters and spent one semester at Hardin Simmons University in Abilene, Texas. During those first years of college, he answered God's call to the ministry and finished his early years of education at Criswell Bible College in Dallas. In May of 1979, Bobby graduated from Criswell with a BA degree in Biblical studies.

While going to Criswell, Bobby was asked to lead the music at FBC of Sunnyvale. It is there that he met a beautiful young lady who would one day be his wife. Kim and Bobby got married on May 12, 1979, the day before his college graduation. Two weeks later, they were serving in Slaton, Texas. Bobby served as the music and youth director of Westview Baptist Church. Jim Wilkerson, who had been Bobby's pastor as a teenager in Big Spring, was the pastor there. (He is a "retired" preacher now and is an active member of Bobby's church today!)

In June of 1981, Bobby and Kim moved to Sulphur Springs, Texas, where Bobby served as pastor of Trinity Baptist Church for seven years. While in Sulphur Springs, the Lord blessed them with their first three children: Amy, Nathan, and Stacy.

In June of 1988 and with Kim being eight months pregnant with their fourth and final child (Julie), the family moved to the very top of the Panhandle of Texas—Perryton, Texas, to be exact. Bobby served as the pastor of Southside Baptist Church there for over eleven years.

In July of 2000, God called Bobby to his present pastorate—Calvary Baptist Church in San Angelo, Texas. (At the writing of this book, he has served there over seventeen years.) It is during this time that he went back to college. He would be a part of the online studies of Liberty University out of Lynchburg, Virginia. Taking several years to complete his education, Bobby receive an MDiv degree as well as an MAR degree. He followed that up with a DMin degree which he received in May of 2017. The area of specific studies at Liberty University was in Expository Preaching and Evangelism.

Kim and Bobby's children are all grown now and they are the proud grandparents of seven grandchildren. He has authored one other book, *The Lost Art of Revivals*. This is the book form of his dissertation work at Liberty University and is available on Amazon. He can be contacted through his email at calvarypreacher@hotmail.com.

Made in the USA
Columbia, SC
17 June 2024

37249607R00055